November

Making Books with Pockets

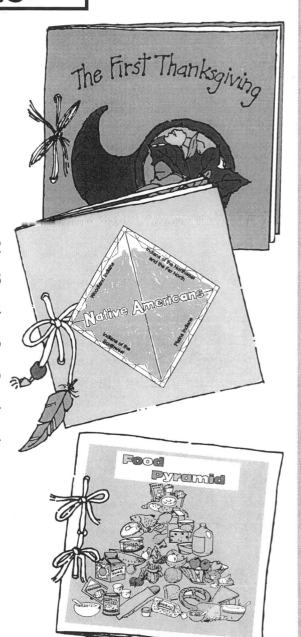

The series of monthly activity books you've been waiting for!

Enliven every month of the year with fun, exciting learning projects that students can proudly present in a unique book format.

Each month has lessons for art, writing, reading, math, science, social studies, and poetry.

Michelle Barnett, Caitlin Rabanera, and **Ann Switzer** have taught first, second, and third grade. Their teaching experiences have involved working with limited-English-speaking students from many parts of the world, supervising student teachers, and conducting inservice sessions for colleagues. They are currently teaching in Southern California.

Congratulations on your purchase of some of the finest teaching materials in the world.

For information about other Evan-Moor products, call 1-800-777-4362 or FAX 1-800-777-4332

Visit our website http://www.evan-moor.com. Check the Product Updates link for supplements, additions, and corrections for this book.

Authors: Michelle Barnett
Caitlin Rabanera
Ann Switzer
Additional Material: Jill Norris
Editor: Marilyn Evans
Copy Editor: Cathy Harbor
Illustrator: Jo Larsen
Designer: Cheryl Puckett
Desktop: Shannon Frederickson

Evan-Moor
EDUCATIONAL PUBLISHERS

EMC 594

Here are ideas for celebrating some of the other special days in November.

November 6_____**James Naismith's Birthday**
Who is James Naismith? He's the man who invented the game of basketball.
In 1891 he decided that there needed to be an active winter game that could be
played indoors. The first basketball game was played with a soccer ball and
peach basket "hoops." Celebrate Mr. Naismith's birthday by shooting baskets and
dribbling basketballs on your playground or have a contest indoors with a trash
can and balls made from wadded-up scrap paper.

November 9_____**Remember Smokey Day**
The first Smokey the Bear was found as a cub clinging to a charred tree after a
New Mexico forest fire in 1950. After his burned paws healed, he lived in the
National Zoo until November 9, 1976, when he died peacefully in his sleep.
Today, a new Smokey continues to pose for posters and advertisements,
reminding people, "Only you can prevent forest fires." Smokey has his own
zip code—20252. Celebrate this day by sending him a letter.

Fourth Monday in November_____**Onion Festival**
In Berne, Switzerland, piles of onions mark the celebration of the Onion Festival.
Costumed people with big onion-head masks march through the streets. Think of
all the ways that you use onions. Try nibbling a few onion rings or enjoying a bowl
of onion soup.

Second Week of November_____**National Split Pea Soup Week**
Enjoy a warm bowl of split pea soup as you read the account of how Owl invited
winter into his home in *Owl at Home* by Arnold Lobel (Harpercrest, 1987).

Peanut Butter Lover's Month
Tally the number of students in your classroom that love peanut butter. Cook
a different peanut butter treat each week. Since the Earl of Sandwich (John
Montagu) was born on November 3, 1718, you might want to start with the
tried-and-true peanut butter sandwich. It is said that Montagu invented the
sandwich in 1762 when he asked that meat be served between two slices of
bread to save the time of using a fork.

November

Sunday	Monday	Tuesday	Wednesday	Thursday	Friday	Saturday

Making Books with Pockets • November • EMC 594

How to Make Pocket Books

Each pocket book has a cover and three or more pockets. Choose construction paper colors that are appropriate to the theme of the book. Using several colors in a book creates an effective presentation.

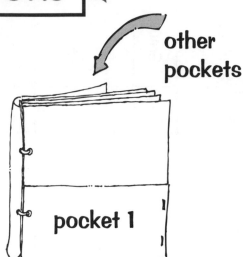

other pockets

pocket 1

Materials

- 12" x 18" (30.5 x 45.5 cm) piece of construction paper for each pocket
- cover as described for each book
- hole punch
- stapler
- string, ribbon, twine, raffia, etc., for ties

Steps to Follow

1. Fold the construction paper to create a pocket. After folding, the paper should measure 12" (30.5 cm) square.

2. Staple the right side of each pocket closed.

3. Punch two or three holes in the left side of each pocket and the cover.

4. Fasten the book together using your choice of material as ties.

5. Glue the poem or information strips onto each pocket as shown on the overview pages of each book.

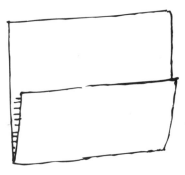

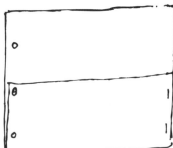

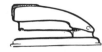

The First Thanksgiving

The Pilgrims who sailed to America in 1620 celebrated their first harvest as many people throughout history have—they had a harvest feast. Learn more about the Pilgrims' journey across the sea, their difficult first year, and their special harvest celebration with this pocket book.

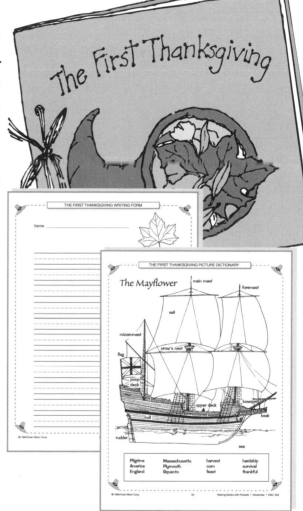

The First Thanksgiving
Book Overview _____ **pages 6 and 7**
These pages show and tell what is in each pocket.

Cover Design _____ **pages 8–10**

Pocket Projects _____ **pages 11–29**
Step-by-step directions and patterns for the activities that go in each pocket.

Pocket Labels _____ **pages 30–32**
This poem can also be used for pocket chart activities throughout the month:
- Chant the poem
- Listen for rhyming words
- Learn new vocabulary
- Identify sight words
- Put words or lines in the correct order

Picture Dictionary _____ **page 33**
Use the picture dictionary to introduce new vocabulary and as a spelling reference. Students can add new pictures, labels, and descriptive adjectives to the pages as their vocabulary increases.

Writing Form _____ **page 34**
Use this form for story writing or as a place to record additional vocabulary words.

BIBLIOGRAPHY

1, 2, 3, Thanksgiving! by W. Nikola-Lisa; Albert Whitman & Co., 1996.
Albert's Thanksgiving by Leslie Tryon; Atheneum, 1994.
The First Thanksgiving by Jean Craighead George; Paper Star, 1996.
Gracias, the Thanksgiving Turkey by Joy Crowley; Scholastic Trade, 1996.
Molly's Pilgrim by Barbara Cohen; Lothrop Lee & Shepard, 1998.
Over the River and Through the Wood by Lydia Maria Child; North South Books, 1998.
The Pilgrims' First Thanksgiving by Ann McGovern; Scholastic Trade, 1993.
The Story of the Pilgrims by Katharine K. Ross; Random House, 1995.
Thanksgiving Is… by Louise Borden; Cartwheel Books, 1997.
Turkey Pox by Laurie Halse Anderson; Albert Whitman & Co., 1998.

POCKET 1

Mayflower Facts pages 11 and 12
Read this minibook with your students to learn more about the Pilgrims' trip across the Atlantic.

Mayflower Model pages 13 and 14
Imagine sharing tiny living quarters with 140 others for 9½ weeks. This cross-section model of the Mayflower will help your students understand how crowded the Mayflower was.

What Will You Take? page 15
"Pack" your most treasured possessions in into this trunk.

The Pilgrims' Path to the New World pages 16 and 17
Trace the Pilgrims' path to America with this map.

A Compact pages 18 and 19
Promote cooperation and teamwork as you write a compact for your classroom.

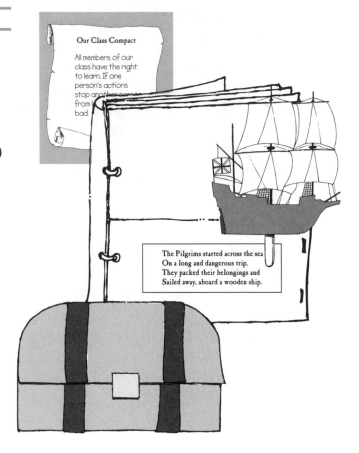

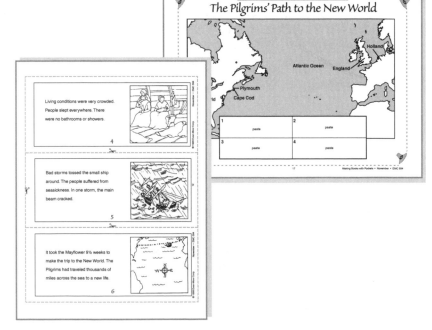

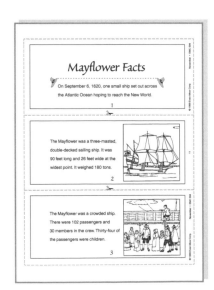

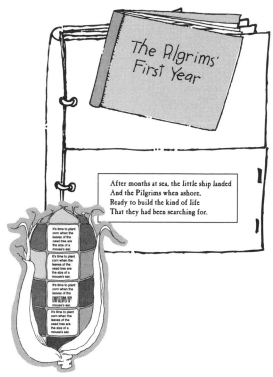

POCKET 2

The Pilgrims' First Year   pages 20–22

This back-to-back book encourages higher-level thinking as students compare their lives with the lives of the Pilgrims.

How to Plant Corn   pages 23–25

Make this corn-shaped poster to remember the important directions that Squanto gave to the Pilgrims.

POCKET 3

Thanksgiving Dinner Placemat   pages 26 and 27

This harvest placemat is also a comparison between the first Thanksgiving dinner and Thanksgiving dinners today.

A Thanksgiving Turkey   pages 28 and 29

This perky turkey will remind students of the facts they have learned about the first Thanksgiving.

Materials

- orange, 12" (30.5 cm) square of construction paper
- cornucopia pattern on page 9, reproduced on brown construction paper for each student
- real pressed leaves or leaf patterns from page 10, reproduced on white construction paper for each student
- glue
- scissors
- black marking pen
- crayons or colored marking pens

Steps to Follow

1. Write "The First Thanksgiving" on the top of the cover.

2. Crumple the cornucopia pattern. Flatten the page and cut out the cornucopia. Glue the cornucopia to the cover.

3. Glue the leaves in place. (If using leaf patterns, color them and cut them out. Then glue them in place.)

Cornucopia Pattern

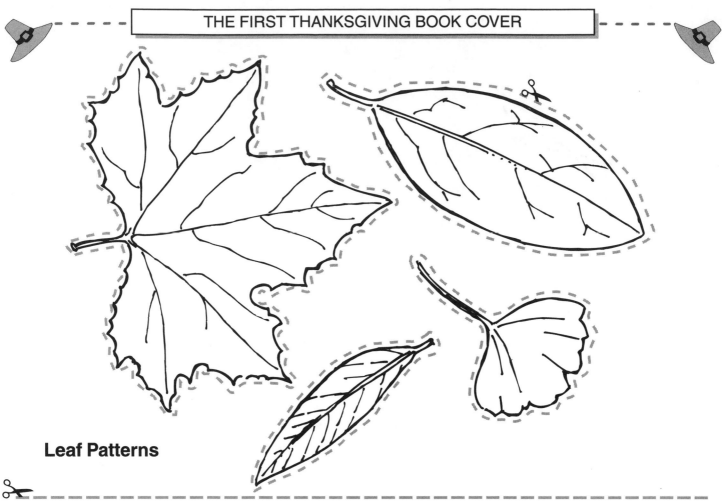

Leaf Patterns

Mayflower Facts

On September 6, 1620, one small ship set out across the Atlantic Ocean hoping to reach the New World.

1

November • EMC 594

© 1999 Evan-Moor Corp.

The Mayflower was a three-masted, double-decked sailing ship. It was 90 feet (27 m) long and 26 feet (8 m) wide at the widest point. It weighed 180 tons (162 metric tonnes).

2

November • EMC 594

© 1999 Evan-Moor Corp.

The Mayflower was a crowded ship. There were 102 passengers and 30 members in the crew. Thirty-four of the passengers were children.

3

November • EMC 594

© 1999 Evan-Moor Corp.

Living conditions were very crowded. People slept everywhere. There were no bathrooms or showers.

4

November • EMC 594

Bad storms tossed the small ship around. The people suffered from seasickness. In one storm, the main beam cracked.

5

November • EMC 594

It took the Mayflower 9½ weeks to make the trip to the New World. The Pilgrims had traveled thousands of miles across the sea to a new life.

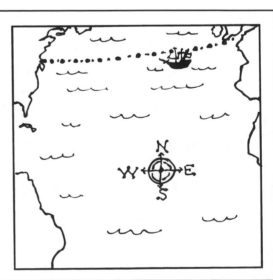

6

November • EMC 594

Mayflower Model

Before making this model of the Mayflower, draw a line 90 feet long (27 meters) on the playground so that students can see the actual length of the Mayflower. Measure your classroom or gym and compare the Mayflower to this room. Talk with your students about how they would like to spend 9½ weeks confined to the small living quarters of the Mayflower.

Materials

- Mayflower pattern on page 14 and interior cross section below, reproduced for each student
- old file folder
- tongue depressor or craft stick
- scissors
- crayons or marking pens
- tape

Steps to Follow

1. Color the ship and the interior cross section. Cut out the two pieces.

2. Glue the ship to the file folder. Trim the edges.

3. Attach the ship to a tongue depressor.

4. Position the cross section on the back of the ship and glue it in place.

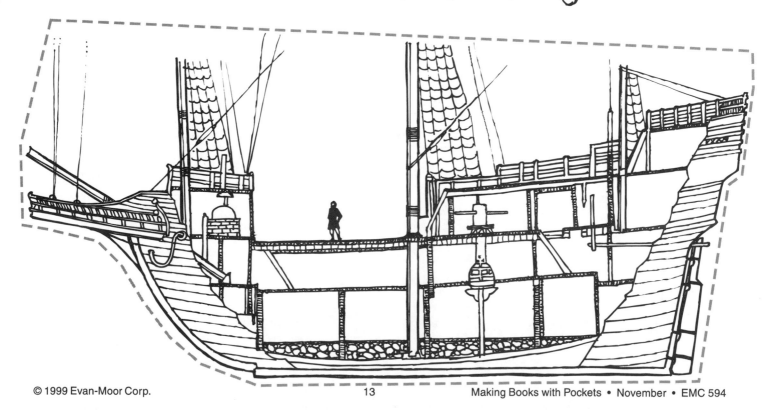

Making Books with Pockets • November • EMC 594

Mayflower Pattern

What Will You Take?

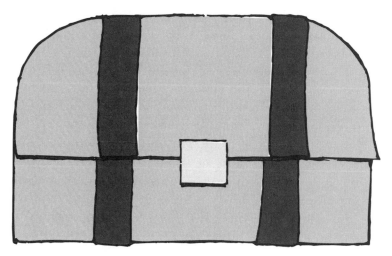

The Mayflower was not large, so the Pilgrims could take only those items that they could not make for themselves or that they needed the first year. They took tools, weapons, and household utensils. They took spinning wheels, looms, cradles for the babies, trade goods, some clothing, seed grains, and garden seeds. Many people took their family Bibles.

Have your students imagine that they are traveling to a new life in a new world. What possessions would they take with them?

Materials

- construction paper
  trunk—brown, 12" x 18" (30.5 x 45.5 cm)
  latch—yellow, 1½" (3.5 cm) square
  straps—black, 1" x 18" (2.5 x 45.5 cm)

- writing paper—6" x 10" (15 x 25.5 cm)
- scissors
- marking pens or crayons
- glue

Steps to Follow

1. Fold the brown paper as shown. Round the top corners to make a trunk shape.

2. Glue the latch to the center of the top flap.

3. Glue the straps to the trunk. Fold the straps around the top and bottom edges.

4. Glue writing paper to the inside of the trunk. List and draw the things that you would take on a long journey to a new life.

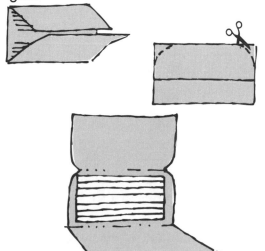

The Pilgrims' Path to the New World

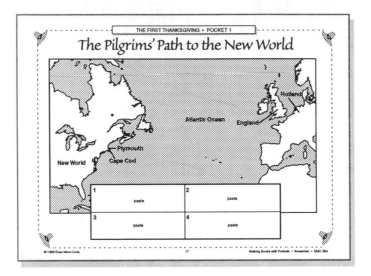

Help your students to understand the path that the Pilgrims took on their journey to the new world with this map project.

Materials

- map pattern on page 17 and the captions below, reproduced for each student
- crayons

Steps to Follow

1. Read the captions. Cut them out and glue them in the boxes on the map.

2. With a crayon, draw the Pilgrims' path on the map.

---

1 The Pilgrims left England to live in Holland.

2 The Pilgrims went back to England to gather supplies for their trip to the New World.

3 After a long ocean journey, the Pilgrims landed at Provincetown Harbor, at the end of Cape Cod.

4 The Pilgrims sailed on to a place they named Plymouth.

The Pilgrims' Path to the New World

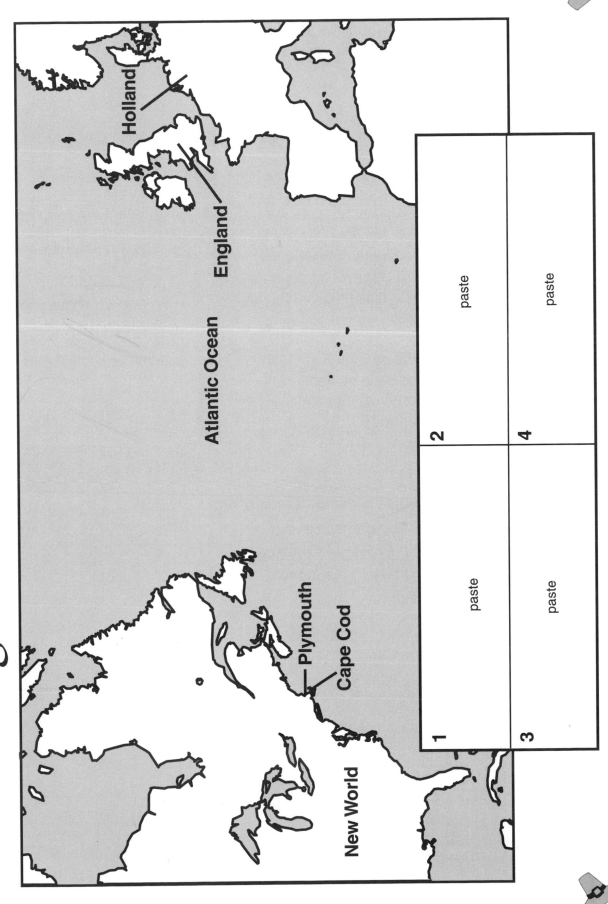

Holland

England

Atlantic Ocean

Plymouth

Cape Cod

New World

1	2
paste	paste
3	4
paste	paste

Making Books with Pockets • November • EMC 594

A Compact

When the Pilgrims landed in Provincetown Harbor, the Pilgrim leaders met and wrote laws called the Mayflower Compact. They believed that they needed to work together in order to succeed. The Pilgrim men agreed on the laws that they would follow and signed the compact.

Write a compact for your classroom or playground. Discuss the "fair" rules that all class members must follow in order to have a well-functioning community.

Our Class Compact

All members of our class have the right to learn. If one person's actions stop another person from learning, that's bad.

Materials

- "Our Class Compact" writing form on page 19, reproduced for each student on parchment or tan construction paper
- brown butcher paper, 10" x 14" (25.5 x 35.5 cm)

Steps to Follow

1. Copy the class compact onto the compact writing form.

2. Glue the form to the butcher paper scroll.

3. Sign the scroll. You may want to have every member of the class sign one scroll to post in the room.

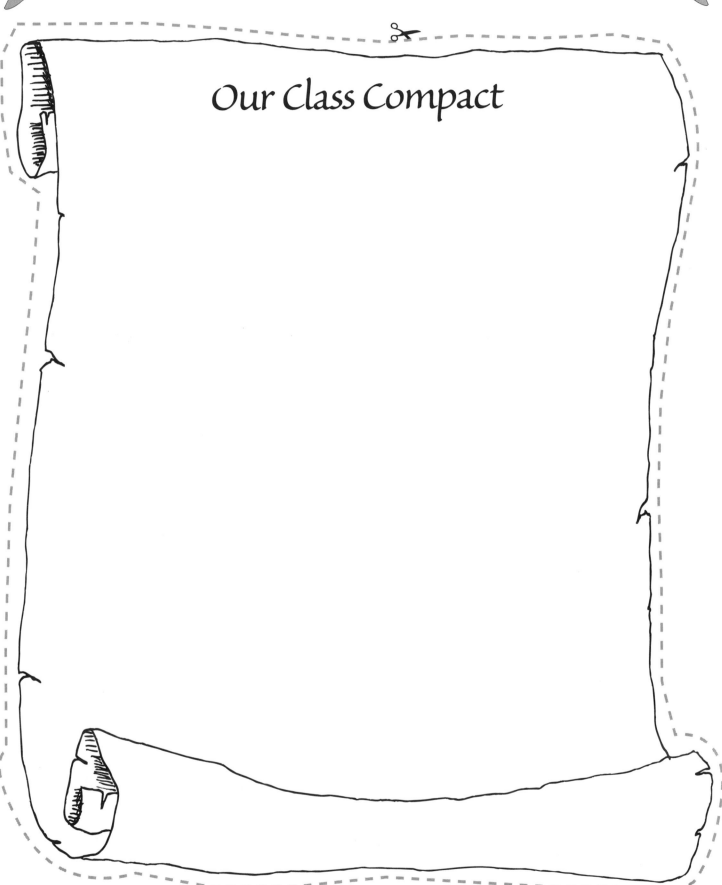

Our Class Compact

The Pilgrims' First Year
A Book of Comparisons

Create this back-to-back book to help your students compare their lives to the lives of the Pilgrims during that first year at Plymouth.

Materials

- book pages on pages 21 and 22, reproduced on white construction paper for each student
- construction paper
  book cover—two 6" x 9" (15 x 23 cm)
  binding strip—2" x 4½" (5 x 11 cm)
- stapler
- glue
- crayons or marking pens

Steps to Follow

1. Cut out "The Pilgrims' First Year" pages. Staple them together in order between the cover pages.

2. Write "The Pilgrims' First Year" on the front cover.

3. Fold the binding strip and glue in place.

4. Read the story about life in Plymouth. Talk about how your students' lives are different than the lives of the Pilgrims.

5. Flip the book over. Write "My Year" on the back cover.

6. Have students write and draw on the backs of the pages to show how their daily lives are different than those of the Pilgrims. Students should write about each aspect of lifestyle mentioned.

The Pilgrims' First Year

1

Houses

The Pilgrims built houses of sawed pine boards. The roofs were thatched. Most houses had just one room. Against one wall was a large fireplace. The fireplace was made of wood covered with clay. The Pilgrims had no bricks and no time to gather stones for stone fireplaces. By April there were seven little houses along a rough road.

> Draw a Pilgrim house.

Making Books with Pockets • November • EMC 594

© 1999 Evan-Moor Corp.

Clothes

2

The Pilgrims wore simple clothes. On weekdays the men wore gray, brown, or blue linen shirts and woolen or leather breeches. When it was cold, they wore sleeveless leather jackets and wool stocking caps. The women wore dresses with full skirts that reached their ankles. In cold weather they wore cloaks with hoods. For the first few years in the Plymouth Colony there were no stores to buy cloth to make new clothes. The women patched and mended the clothes they had brought with them.

> Draw something a Pilgrim might have worn.

Making Books with Pockets • November • EMC 594

© 1999 Evan-Moor Corp.

Jobs and Chores

The Pilgrims worked very hard. They made houses and furniture. They planted gardens and hunted for food. They made soap and candles. Everyone had a job. Young children pulled weeds, gathered nuts and berries, picked up kindling, and rocked cradles. Older children helped with spinning, weaving, pounding corn, making soap, cutting trees, fishing, and hunting.

Draw a chore done by a Pilgrim child.

© 1999 Evan-Moor Corp.　Making Books with Pockets • November • EMC 594

Transportation

The Pilgrims came to Plymouth on the Mayflower. A smaller boat, a shallop, brought the Pilgrims to the shore. They did not have any other means of transportation. They walked everywhere. When the Mayflower sailed back to England, the Pilgrims were on their own in the new land.

Draw a way Pilgrims traveled.

© 1999 Evan-Moor Corp.　Making Books with Pockets • November • EMC 594

How to Plant Corn

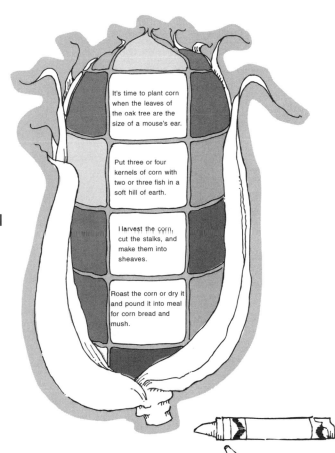

The first corn seeds that the Pilgrims found were buried in a basket under the sand on Cape Cod. Corn was new to the Pilgrims. Their friend, Squanto, taught them how to plant the corn. This lesson was important to their survival.

Make this special ear of corn with "kernels" of wisdom for a successful corn crop.

Materials

- ear of corn pattern on page 24 and kernel patterns on page 25, reproduced for each student
- 9" x 12" (23 x 30.5 cm) yellow construction paper
- marking pens or crayons
- scissors
- glue

Steps to Follow

1. Cut out the ear of corn and the kernels.

2. Glue the ear of corn to the yellow construction paper. Trim the construction paper so that there is a ½" (1.5 cm) border of yellow around the ear.

3. Sequence the kernels and glue them to the appropriate spaces on the ear of corn so that they are in order.

4. Color the remaining kernel spaces with red, yellow, blue, green, and black.

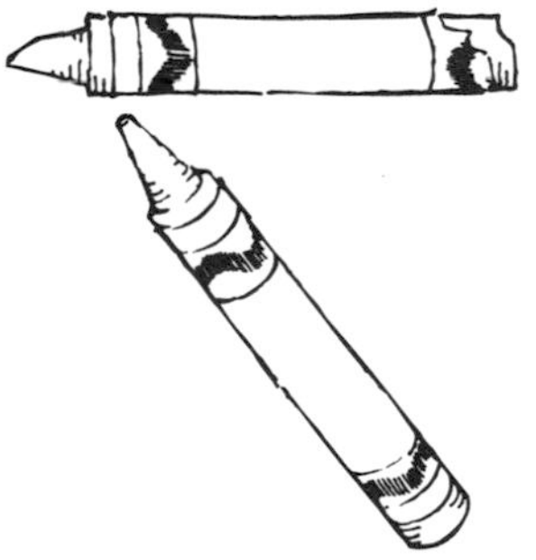

The text inside the illustration:

It's time to plant corn when the leaves of the oak tree are the size of a mouse's ear.

Put three or four kernels of corn with two or three fish in a soft hill of earth.

Harvest the corn, cut the stalks, and make them into sheaves.

Roast the corn or dry it and pound it into meal for corn bread and mush.

Ear of Corn Pattern

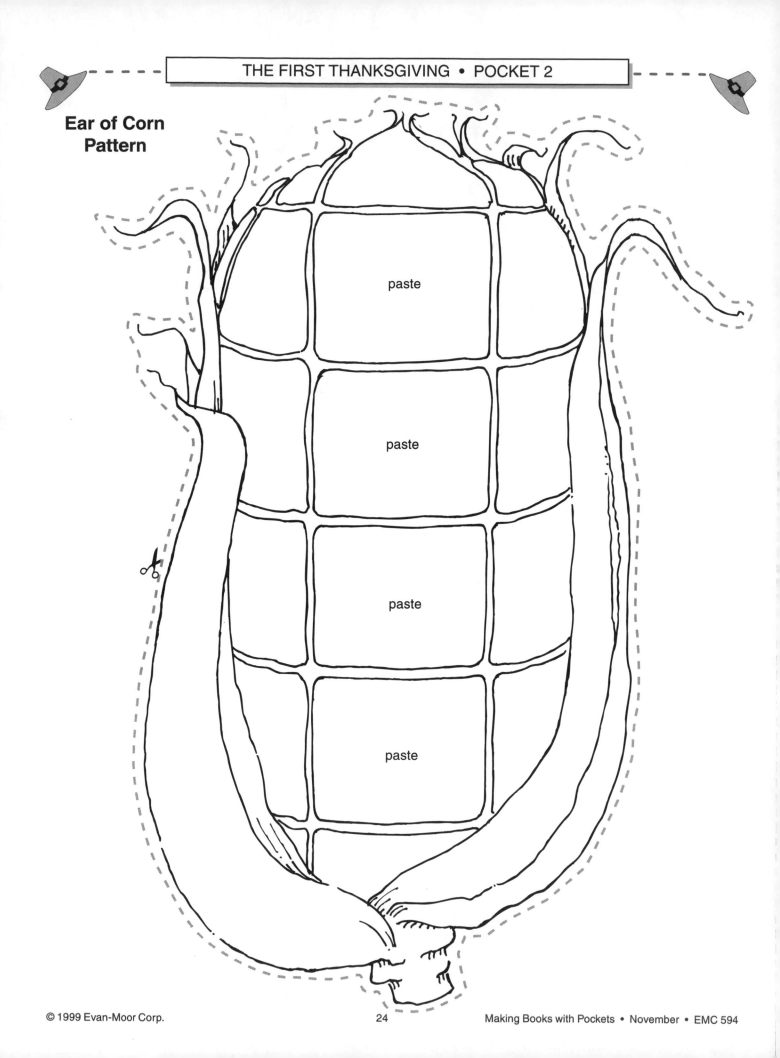

paste

paste

paste

paste

Kernel Patterns

Roast the corn or dry it and pound it into meal for corn bread and mush.

Harvest the corn, cut the stalks, and make them into sheaves.

It's time to plant corn when the leaves of the oak tree are the size of a mouse's ear.

Put three or four kernels of corn with two or three fish in a soft hill of earth.

Roast the corn or dry it and pound it into meal for corn bread and mush.

Harvest the corn, cut the stalks, and make them into sheaves.

It's time to plant corn when the leaves of the oak tree are the size of a mouse's ear.

Put three or four kernels of corn with two or three fish in a soft hill of earth.

Roast the corn or dry it and pound it into meal for corn bread and mush.

Harvest the corn, cut the stalks, and make them into sheaves.

It's time to plant corn when the leaves of the oak tree are the size of a mouse's ear.

Put three or four kernels of corn with two or three fish in a soft hill of earth.

Thanksgiving Dinner Placemat

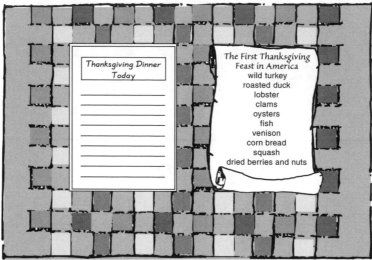

Thanksgiving Dinner Today

The First Thanksgiving Feast in America
wild turkey
roasted duck
lobster
clams
oysters
fish
venison
corn bread
squash
dried berries and nuts

Compare the first Thanksgiving feast with a modern Thanksgiving dinner as you make a colorful woven placemat. Read accounts of the first Thanksgiving. Ask your students who attended the Pilgrim harvest celebration. Then talk with your students about who comes to their Thanksgiving dinners today. Discuss the foods that they eat. Work with your class to make a Thanksgiving Dinner Word Bank for reference as students fill in their modern-day menus.

Materials

- menu patterns on page 27, reproduced for each student
- construction paper
  placemat—orange, 12" x 18" (30.5 x 45.5 cm)
  weaving strips—yellow, light brown, red, and brown, 12" x 1" (30.5 x 2.5 cm)

- pencil
- scissors
- glue

Steps to Follow

1. Make the placemat.
   - Fold the orange paper in half.
   - Cut slits from the fold to about 1" (2.5 cm) from edge. Slits should be about 1" (2.5 cm) apart.
   - Unfold the paper.
   - Weave yellow, brown, and red strips through the slits.
   - Glue the ends of the strips to the orange placemat to hold them in place.

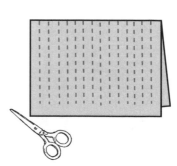

2. Cut out the menu patterns.

3. Fill in the modern-day menu.

4. Glue the menus to the placemat.

5. Laminate the placemat.

         Making Books with Pockets • November • EMC 594

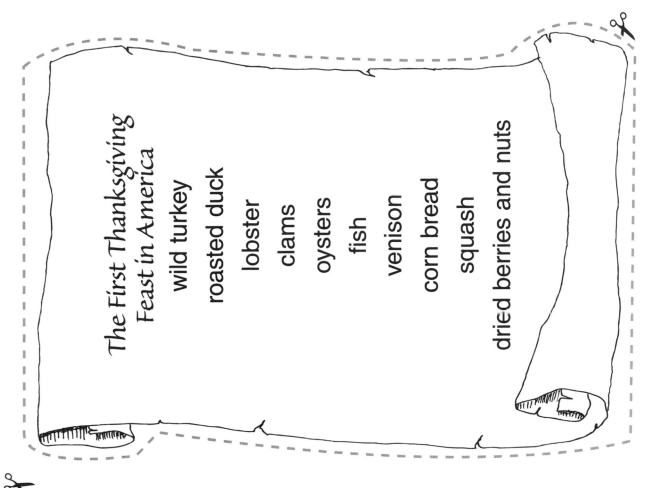

The First Thanksgiving
Feast in America

wild turkey

roasted duck

lobster

clams

oysters

fish

venison

corn bread

squash

dried berries and nuts

Thanksgiving Dinner
Today

A Thanksgiving Turkey

Write facts about the first Thanksgiving on each feather of this proud bird.

Materials

- construction paper
  body—pattern on page 29,
    reproduced on brown for each
    student
  feet—yellow scraps
  feathers—assorted colors, *cut from scraps*
    2" x 6" (5 x 15 cm)
- thin black marking pen
- scissors
- crayons
- 1½" (3.5 cm) brown tissue paper squares
- glue *little paper nut cups*
- pencil

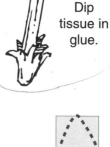

Steps to Follow

1. Cut out the turkey body.

2. Cut two feet from the yellow scraps. Glue them to the body.

3. Wrap one piece of tissue paper around the eraser end of the pencil. Dip the end into the glue and press it onto the turkey body.

4. Color the eyes and beak.

5. Cut feathers from the assorted colored strips.

6. Write a fact about the first Thanksgiving on the back of each feather.

7. Glue the feathers to the turkey body. The facts should be on the back.

8. Use a black crayon to make feather lines on the front of each feather.

Dip tissue in glue.

Cut out feathers.

Turkey Pattern

Making Books with Pockets • November • EMC 594

Note: Reproduce this page and pages 31 and 32 to label each of the three pockets of the Thanksgiving book.

Pocket 1

The Pilgrims started across the sea

On a long and dangerous trip.

They packed their belongings and

Sailed away, aboard a wooden ship.

Making Books with Pockets • November • EMC 594

Pocket 2

After months at sea, the little ship landed
And the Pilgrims went ashore,
Ready to build the kind of life
That they had been searching for.

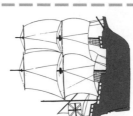

Pocket 3

At the end of a year the few that survived
Gave thanks for all they had.
For harvest of plenty and friends who were kind,
The Pilgrims prayed and were glad.

The Mayflower

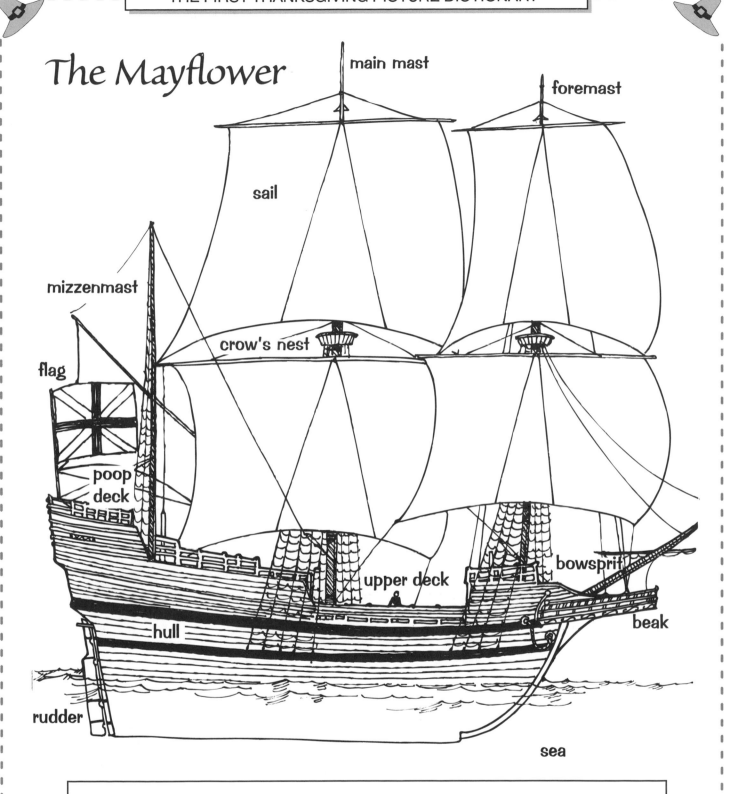

main mast

foremast

sail

mizzenmast

crow's nest

flag

poop deck

bowsprit

upper deck

beak

hull

rudder

sea

Pilgrims	Massachusetts	harvest	hardship
America	Plymouth	corn	survival
England	Squanto	feast	thankful

Name: _____

Native Americans

Several million people lived in North America before the arrival of Europeans. These people believed that the land was for everyone to use and share. Some of the people were hunters and others were farmers. The Native Americans called themselves by the names of their tribes. There were hundreds of tribes in America when Christopher Columbus arrived and thought that he was in India. He called all of the tribes "Indians," even though the people he referred to were scattered all over the country, spoke different languages, and had different customs. This pocket book summarizes the traditions of Native Americans in four different regions.

Native Americans
Book Overview _____ **pages 36–38**
These pages show and tell what is in each pocket.

Cover Design _____ **pages 39 and 40**

Pocket Projects _____ **pages 41–59**
Step-by-step directions and patterns for the activities that go in each pocket.

Pocket Labels _____ **pages 60 and 61**

Picture Dictionary _____ **page 62**
Use the picture dictionary to introduce new vocabulary and as a spelling reference. Students can add new pictures, labels, and descriptive adjectives to the page as their vocabulary increases.

Writing Form _____ **page 63**
Use this form for story writing or as a place to record additional vocabulary words.

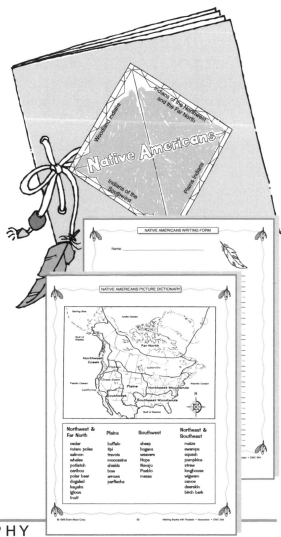

BIBLIOGRAPHY

Brother Eagle, Sister Sky by Chief Seattle; Dial Books, 1991.
Dancing with the Indians by Angela Shelf Medearis; Holiday House, 1993.
Native Americans by Jay Miller; Children's Press, 1994.
Native Americans (First Discovery Book) by Gallimard Jeunesse; Scholastic Trade, 1998.
The Very First Americans by Cara Ashrose; Grosset and Dunlap, 1993.

Additional book references for specific pockets are listed on page 38.

POCKET 1

Information Page   page 41

Use this page about Woodlands Natives for your own information, make it into a transparency to use with your class, and reproduce it for each student.

Cornhusk Mask   page 42

Make a paper plate replica of a cornhusk mask.

Choose a Name for Yourself   pages 43 and 44

Your students will enjoy giving themselves special names that represent their abilities and character traits.

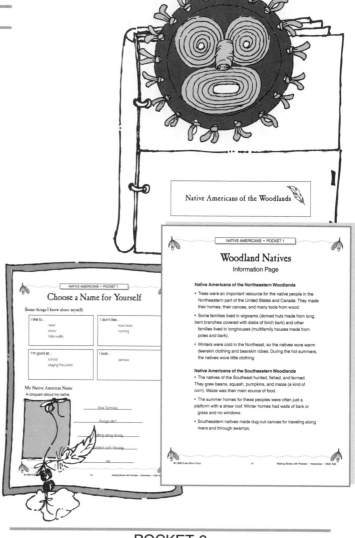

POCKET 2

Information Page   page 45

Use this page about natives of the Great Plains for your own information, make it into a transparency to use with your class, and reproduce it for each student.

Parfleche   pages 46 and 47

Carry homework assignments and information in this replica of a hide envelope used by natives of the Great Plains.

Picture Writing   page 48

Enjoy writing stories without words.

Winter Counts   pages 49 and 50

Draw symbols on a "hide" to represent important events of students' lives.

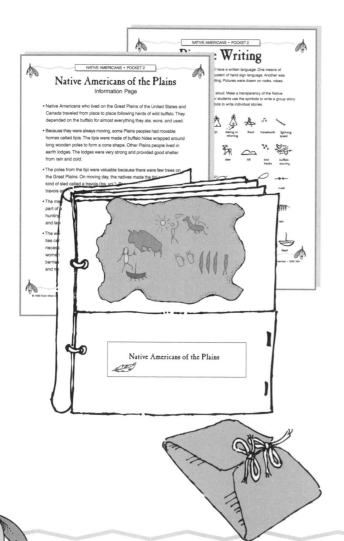

POCKET 3

Information Page   page 51
Use this page about natives of the Southwest for your own information, make it into a transparency to use with your class, and reproduce it for each student.

Weave a Mat   page 52
Use natural materials and enjoy weaving.

Kachina Dolls   pages 53 and 54
Decorate your own spirit rainmaker.

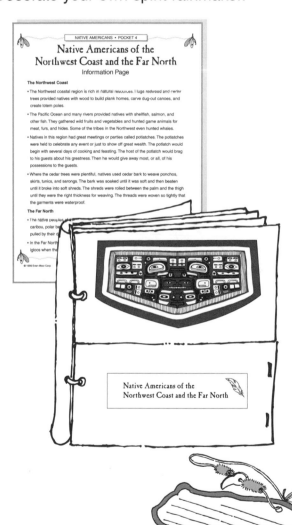

POCKET 4

Information Page   page 55
Use this page about natives of the Northwest Coast and the Far North for your own information, make it into a transparency to use with your class, and reproduce it for each student.

Chilkat Blankets   pages 56 and 57
Talk about symmetry as you work on the designs for this project.

The Courage
of a Hunter   pages 58 and 59
Write about a bear hunt and decorate it with a "bear claw" to honor the courage shown by the hunters.

WOODLAND NATIVES

Corn Is Maize by Aliki; Crowell, 1976.
Dancing Drum by Terri Cohlene; Rourke Corporation, 1990.
Little Firefly by Terri Cohlene; Rourke Corporation, 1990.
The Talking Earth by Jean Craighead George; Harper and Row, 1983.

NATIVES OF THE GREAT PLAINS

Buffalo Woman by Paul Goble; Bradbury Press, 1984.
Death of the Iron Horse by Paul Goble; Bradbury Press, 1986.
Gift of the Sacred Dog by Paul Goble; Bradbury Press, 1980.
If You Lived with the Sioux by Ann McGovern; Four Winds Press, 1974.
Quillworker by Terri Cohlene; Rourke Corporation, 1990.
The Legend of Scarface by Robert San Souci; Doubleday, 1978.
Where the Buffaloes Begin by Olaf Baker; F. Warne, 1981.

NATIVES OF THE SOUTHWEST

Annie and the Old One by Miska Miles; Brown, 1971.
Arrow to the Sun by Gerald McDermott; Viking Press, 1974.
Pueblo Boy: Growing Up in Two Worlds by Marcia Keegan; Cobblehill
    Books, 1991.
The Spider, the Cave, and the Pottery Bowl by Eleanor Clymer;
    Atheneum, 1971.
Turquoise Boy by Terri Cohlene; Rourke Corporation, 1990.

NATIVES OF THE NORTHWEST COAST, CALIFORNIA, AND THE FAR NORTH

Clamshell Boy by Terri Cohlene; Rourke Corporation, 1990.
Ka-ha-si and the Loon by Terri Cohlene; Rourke Corporation, 1990.
Whale in the Sky by Anne Siberell; E. P. Dutton, 1982.

Materials

- yellow, 12" (30.5 cm) square of construction paper
- pattern on page 40, reproduced for each student
- crayons
- black watercolor paint
- paintbrush
- glue
- scissors
- roving
- beads and feathers

Steps to Follow

1. Color the pattern. Fill in the letters with a light color.

2. Cover with a black watercolor wash. Let the paint dry completely.

3. Cut the pattern out and glue it to the yellow cover.

4. Tie the book pages together with heavy roving. Decorate the ends of the roving with beads and feathers.

Cover Pattern

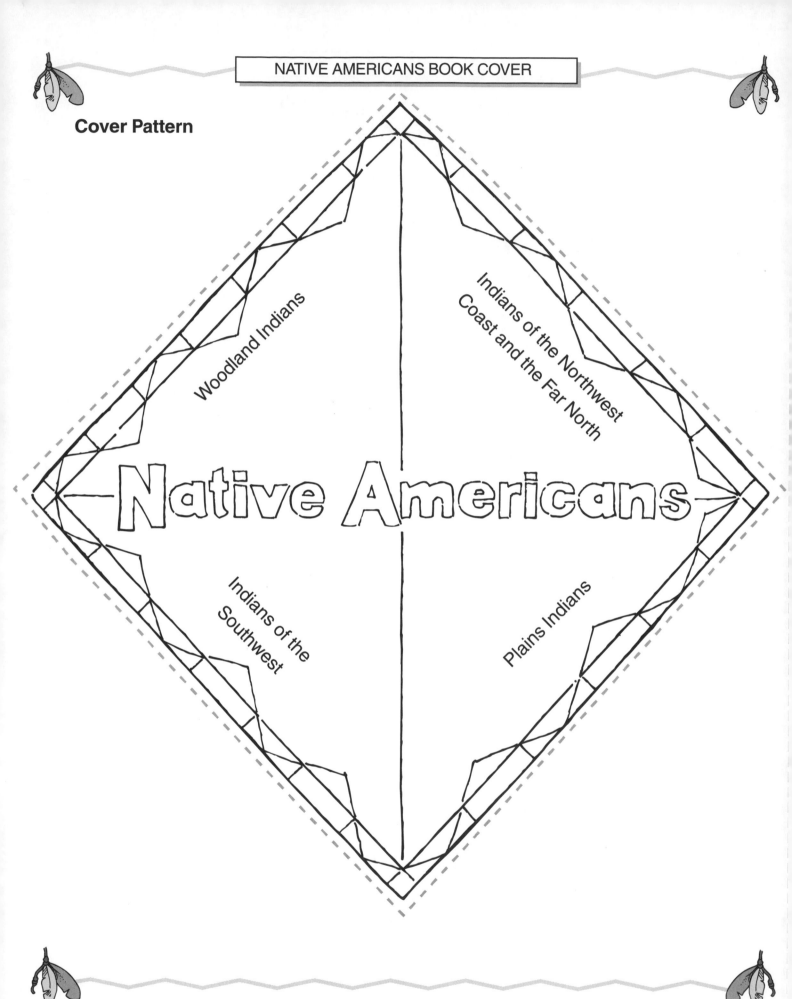

Woodland Indians

Indians of the Northwest Coast and the Far North

Native Americans

Indians of the Southwest

Plains Indians

Woodland Natives
Information Page

Native Americans of the Northeastern Woodlands

• Trees were an important resource for the native people in the Northeastern part of the United States and Canada. They made their homes, their canoes, and many tools from wood.

• Some families lived in wigwams (domed huts made from long, bent branches covered with slabs of birch bark) and other families lived in longhouses (multifamily houses made from poles and bark).

• Winters were cold in the Northeast, so the natives wore warm deerskin clothing and bearskin robes. During the hot summers, the natives wore little clothing.

Native Americans of the Southeastern Woodlands

• The natives of the Southeast hunted, fished, and farmed. They grew beans, squash, pumpkins, and maize (a kind of corn). Maize was their main source of food.

• The summer homes for these peoples were often just a platform with a straw roof. Winter homes had walls of bark or grass and no windows.

• Southeastern natives made dug-out canoes for traveling along rivers and through swamps.

Cornhusk Mask

Woodland Indians sometimes wore cornhusk masks as they performed traditional dances. This mask looks something like theirs.

Materials

- a black paper plate
- dried cornhusks, cut into 8" (20 cm) strips
- raffia or coarse rug yarn
- glue
- scissors
- paper punch

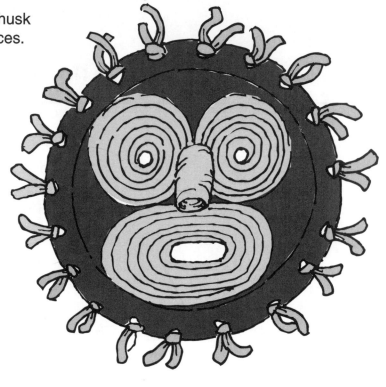

Steps to Follow

1. Cut holes in the paper plate for eyes and mouth. (This step may need to be completed by an adult.)

2. With the paper punch, make holes about 1" (2.5 cm) apart all around the rim of the plate.

3. Coat the area around the eyes and mouth with glue. Coil the raffia around each hole 10 times. Push the raffia firmly into the glue, adding more glue as necessary. The coiled raffia should cover most of the plate.

4. Roll one cornhusk into a tube. Tie it with a thin strip of cornhusk or tape it. Glue the tube onto the mask as the nose.

5. Loop cornhusk strips through the punched holes to make a fringe around the outside edge of the mask.

Step 1   Step 5

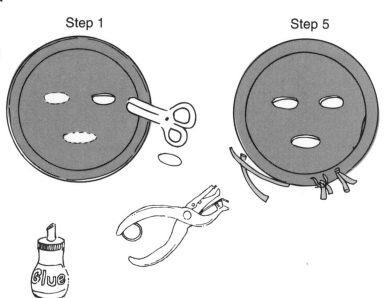

Choose a Name for Yourself

Native American children were given names that represented special qualities, abilities, or personality traits. A wise, observant child might be named "Shining Owl." Your students will enjoy giving themselves Native American names.

Materials

- writing form on page 44, reproduced for each student and as a transparency to use with the class
- brown, 9" x 12" (23 x 30.5 cm) paper—a brown paper bag, poster paper, or construction paper
- brown, 2" x 3" (5 x 7.5 cm) construction paper
- small animal cookies
- beads or feathers
- yarn
- scissors
- hole punch

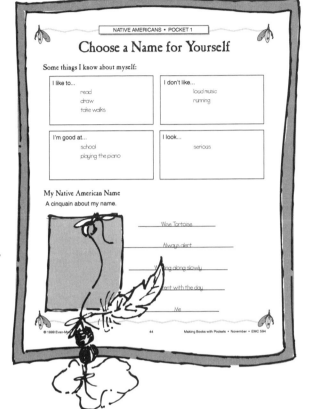

Steps to Follow

1. Model the name-giving process for students:
   - List your abilities or personality traits on the writing form.
   - Think of an animal that shares some of the same characteristics.
   - Add one or two adjectives from your list to the animal's name. This becomes your Native American name.
   - Write a cinquain to tell about the name. The first line of the cinquain will be the name. Use the abilities list as a word bank.

2. Students individually list abilities, choose names, and write cinquains.

3. Mount the writing form on the brown paper.

4. Tie yarn around one animal cookie. Add a bead or a feather. Punch a hole in the brown rectangle and tie on this "fetish." (A fetish is a good luck charm. Native American fetishes were made in the shape of animals and other living things.)

5. Glue the brown rectangle over the directions for the cinquain.

Choose a Name for Yourself

Some things I know about myself:

I like to...	I don't like...
I'm good at...	I look...

My Native American Name

A cinquain about my name.

Line 1—
the Native American name

Line 2—
two words describing the name
(adjectives)

Line 3—
three words expressing action
(verbs)

Line 4—
four words expressing feelings
(nouns)

Line 5—
one word

_____

_____

_____

_____

_____

Native Americans of the Plains
Information Page

- Native Americans who lived on the Great Plains of the United States and Canada traveled from place to place following herds of wild buffalo. They depended on the buffalo for almost everything they ate, wore, and used.

- Because they were always moving, some Plains peoples had movable homes called tipis. The tipis were made of buffalo hides wrapped around long wooden poles to form a cone shape. Other Plains people lived in earth lodges. The lodges were very strong and provided good shelter from rain and cold.

- The poles from the tipi were valuable because there were few trees on the Great Plains. On moving day, the natives made the tipi poles into a kind of sled called a travois (trə voi´). Possessions were loaded on the travois and it was pulled by people, dogs, or horses.

- The men of the Plains tribes were skillful hunters. They never wasted any part of a killed animal. The men also made the tools that they needed for hunting. They made their own bows, arrows, shields, and lances.

- The women of the Plains tribes were honored as the life-givers. Their duties centered around the home and the family. Raising children was necessary for the tribe to survive. After the men hunted the buffalo, the women butchered, cooked, and preserved the meat. They gathered wild berries, fruits, and roots. They tanned hides and sewed all the clothing and moccasins for the family.

Parfleche

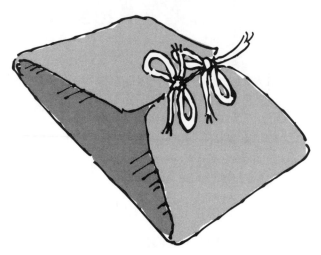

The Plains people made a large envelope out of rawhide to carry dried food and other items. The envelope was called a parfleche.

Make a parfleche to hold special writing projects.

Materials

- parfleche template on page 47, reproduced for each student
- brown paper bag
- two 6" (15 cm) lengths of yarn or cord
- hole punch
- scissors
- marking pens

Steps to Follow

1. Trace the parfleche template onto a brown paper bag.

2. Cut out the parfleche. Punch holes where indicated.

3. Decorate the outside of the parfleche with the marking pens.

4. Put a length of yarn through each pair of holes. The loose ends should be on the decorated side of the parfleche.

5. Fold the parfleche as shown.
   - Fold the two longest sides to the middle.
   - Fold the other two sides together.

6. Tie the ends with the yarn.

To carry something in the parfleche, untie it and open it up. Put the item in, refold, and tie. Use your parfleche to carry special papers or snacks.

Parfleche Template

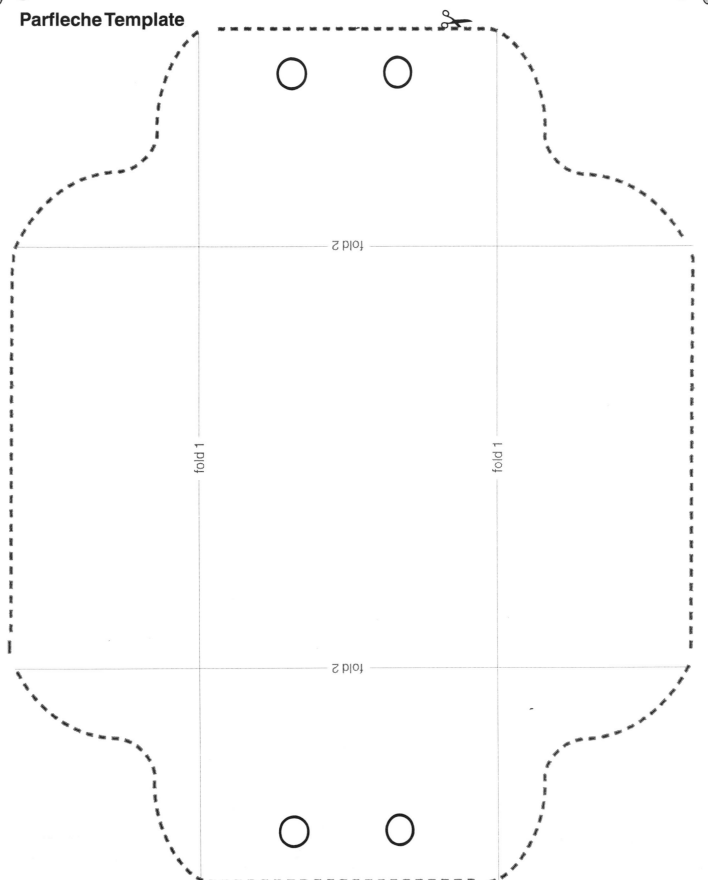

fold 2

fold 1

fold 1

fold 2

Making Books with Pockets • November • EMC 594

Picture Writing

The natives of the Great Plains did not have a written language. One means of communication with others was their system of hand sign language. Another was a system of pictographs, or picture writing. Pictures were drawn on rocks, robes, and tipis.

Read several Native American stories aloud. Make a transparency of the Native American pictographs below. Help your students use the symbols to write a group story. Then have your students use the symbols to write individual stories.

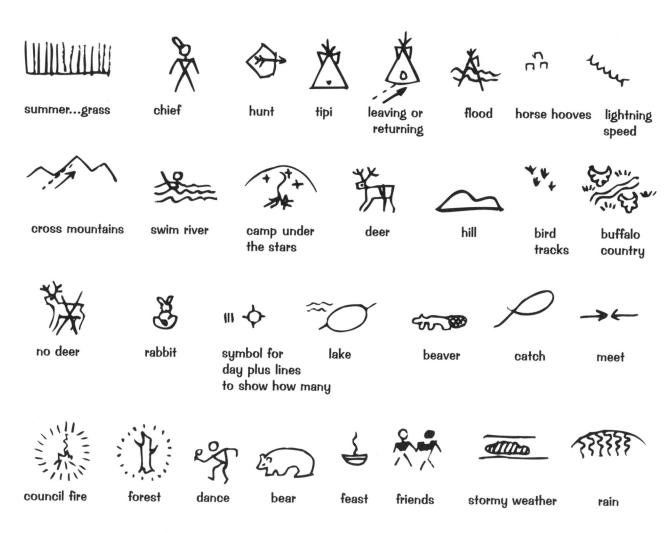

summer...grass   chief   hunt   tipi   leaving or returning   flood   horse hooves   lightning speed

cross mountains   swim river   camp under the stars   deer   hill   bird tracks   buffalo country

no deer   rabbit   symbol for day plus lines to show how many   lake   beaver   catch   meet

council fire   forest   dance   bear   feast   friends   stormy weather   rain

2 days   powwow   hike   meeting in friendship   award   surprise   war   feast

Winter Counts

The Plains people did not have calendars as we know them, but they had an interesting method of keeping track of time. Instead of numbering years, they remembered "winters" by a particular event or situation that occurred during that winter. The winter count would have been painted on buffalo hide. The counts were carefully saved.

Make winter counts to remember special events in your students' lives.

Materials

- hide form on page 50, reproduced for each student
- marking pens
- scissors

Steps to Follow

1. Have students think about the important events in their lives. They should think of one or two for each year.

2. Then have them develop a symbol for each of the events. Draw the symbols on the hide pattern.

3. Students will enjoy sharing their personal winter counts.

You might want to create a year count for your school year. Add symbols for each important event that occurs.

Name: _____

Winter Counts

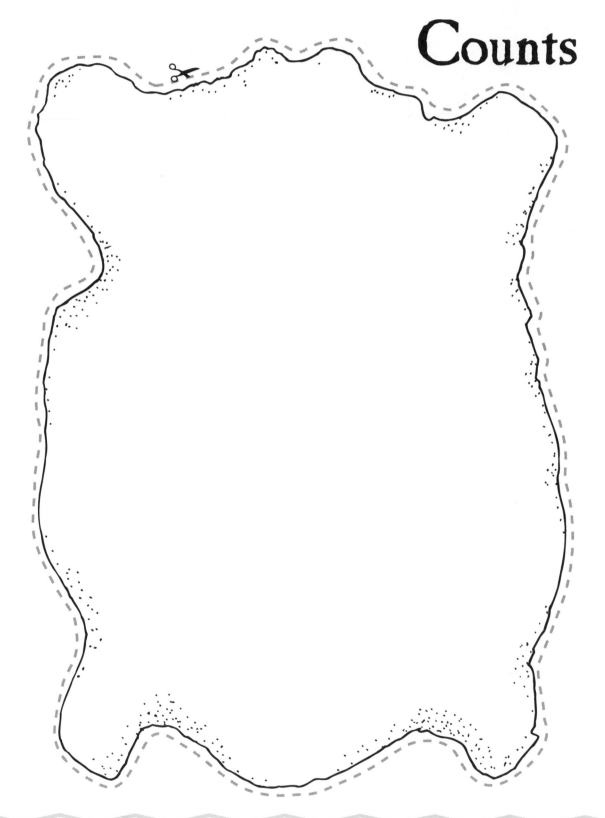

Making Books with Pockets • November • EMC 594

Native Americans of the Southwest

Information Page

- The people of the Southwest lived in a dry, hot climate. They were farmers growing crops of corn, cotton, and squash. They herded sheep and used the wool for rugs and blankets.

- The Navajo people lived in hogans. A hogan is a dome-shaped house made from logs and dirt. The doorway of a hogan always faced east as a sign of respect for the rising sun.

- The Hopi and the Pueblo peoples lived on the top of mesas (flat-topped hills). The Hopi had homes made of rocks and mud. The Pueblo people formed walls out of building blocks made with a mixture of clay, water, and straw. They covered their houses with smooth layers of mud. The buildings were like an apartment house, with different families living on different levels.

- The people of the Southwest were artists known for their baskets, pottery, rugs, jewelry, and blankets.

Weave a Mat

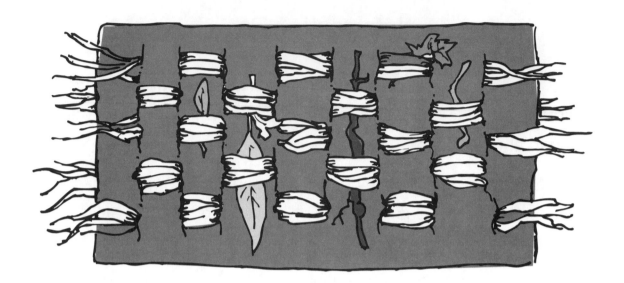

The early natives of the Southwest wove their own mats from the grasses that they gathered. Gather your own natural materials and weave them into a mat.

Materials

- 6" x 10" (15 x 25.5 cm) piece of brown paper bag or felt
- 12" (30.5 cm) lengths of raffia
- natural materials—dried grasses, weeds, cornstalks, cornhusks, leaves, etc.
- scissors

Steps to Follow

1. Fold the rectangular base in half lengthwise.

2. Cut on the fold as shown. Stop about 1" (2.5 cm) from the open edge. Make the cuts about 1½" (4 cm) apart. When the paper is opened, it will form a loom.

3. Take several pieces of raffia and weave the bunch over and under through the slits in the loom. Weave different bunches in new rows to fill the loom.

4. Add bits of dried grasses and other materials.

Kachina Dolls

Kachina dolls represent spirit rainmakers. There are over 200 kachina spirits, each with its own mask. The kachinas are part of ceremonies to bring rain and good fortune.

Materials

- a cardboard tube (from a paper towel or toilet tissue roll)
- kachina mask patterns on page 54, reproduced on construction paper
- bits of colored tissue, construction paper, or thin cloth
- small feathers
- scraps of aluminum foil
- tiny buttons and beads
- toothpicks
- craft sticks
- paint
- colored markers

Steps to Follow

1. Find pictures of kachinas in library books. Show them to students, calling special attention to the large headpieces with geometric shapes.

2. Paint each tube white. Flatten the tube a bit.

3. Draw or paint legs on the bottom part of the tube.

4. Draw or paint arms on the middle part of the tube.

5. Choose a mask pattern. Cut it out. Use paper, feathers, buttons, and other supplies to add features and decorate the mask. Glue it onto the tube.

Kachina Mask Patterns

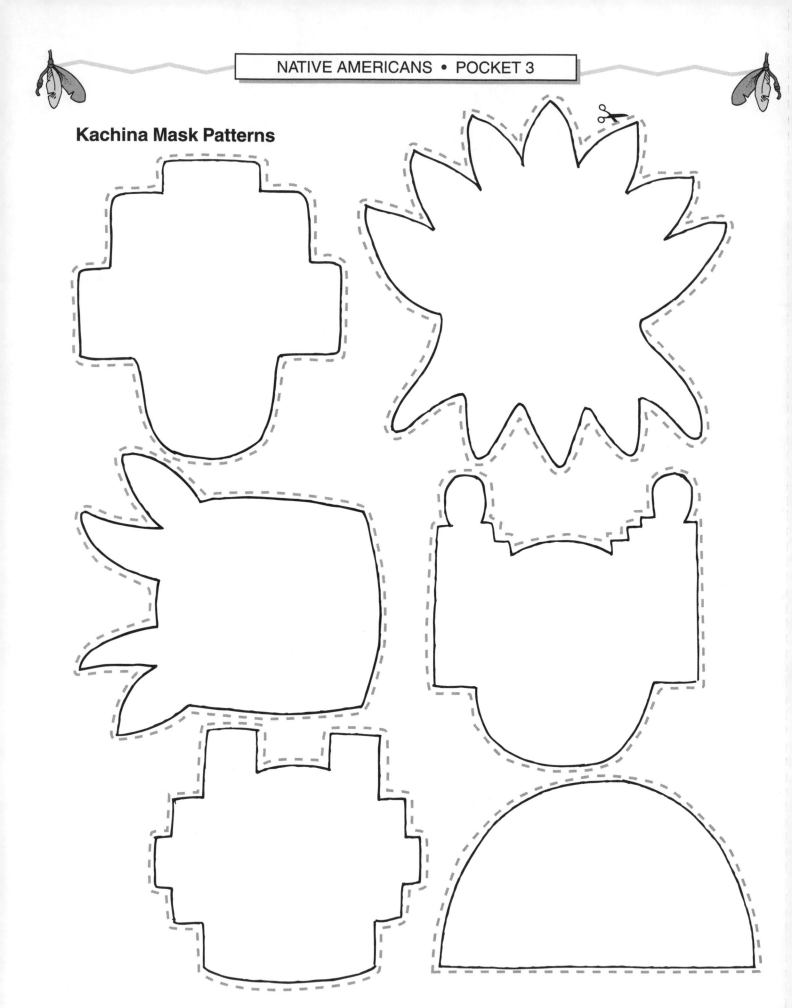

54

Native Americans of the Northwest Coast and the Far North
Information Page

The Northwest Coast

- The Northwest coastal region is rich in natural resources. Huge redwood and cedar trees provided natives with wood to build plank homes, carve dug-out canoes, and create totem poles.

- The Pacific Ocean and many rivers provided natives with shellfish, salmon, and other fish. They gathered wild fruits and vegetables and hunted game animals for meat, furs, and hides. Some of the tribes in the Northwest even hunted whales.

- Natives in this region had great meetings or parties called potlatches. The potlatches were held to celebrate any event or just to show off great wealth. The potlatch would begin with several days of cooking and feasting. The host of the potlatch would brag to his guests about his greatness. Then he would give away most, or all, of his possessions to the guests.

- Where the cedar trees were plentiful, natives used cedar bark to weave ponchos, skirts, tunics, and sarongs. The bark was soaked until it was soft and then beaten until it broke into soft shreds. The shreds were rolled between the palm and the thigh until they were the right thickness for weaving. The threads were woven so tightly that the garments were waterproof.

The Far North

- The native peoples of the Far North lived on fish and sea mammals. They hunted caribou, polar bears, and wolves. They sped across the frozen ground on sleds pulled by their dogs or paddled through icy waters in kayaks.

- In the Far North the natives lived in huts and hide tents. The Canadian Inuit built igloos when they were hunting.

Chilkat Blankets

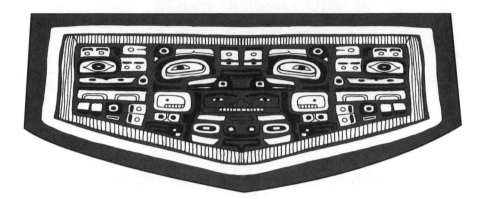

Tlingit and Tsimshian women wove goat's hair with cedar bark to make beautiful blankets worn only by chiefs or persons of high rank. The designs represented parts of fish, birds, or animals. The designs were symmetrical and were woven in shades of yellow, blue, black, and white. The blankets were trimmed with long fringe at the bottom. It was not unusual for women to work longer than a year to make one blanket.

Materials

- Chilkat pattern on page 57, reproduced for each student
- black construction paper—6" x 12" (15 x 30.5 cm)
- yellow and blue crayons
- glue
- scissors

Steps to Follow

1. Color the Chilkat pattern. Make it symmetrical. Then cut it out.

2. Glue the pattern to the black construction paper. Trim around the edges so that there is a small black border.

Chilkat Pattern

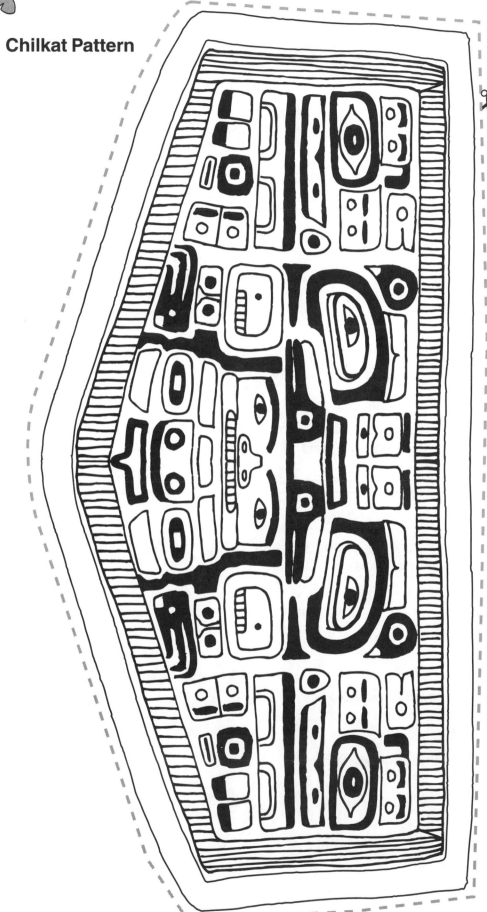

The Courage of a Hunter

Native American hunters who killed a bear often wore the bear's claws as a sign of their courage. Imagine hunting a bear without modern firearms. Read several stories about Native American hunters to your class. Have students write or tell a story describing courage in the hunt. Record the stories on the writing form on page 59. Then reward your "hunters" by attaching bear claws to their stories.

Materials

- foam meat trays
- fake fur, cut in 2" x 3" (5 x 7.5 cm) rectangles
- string or cord
- glue
- scissors
- hole punch
- bear writing form on page 59, reproduced for each student
- brown construction paper—8½" x 11" (21 x 28 cm)

Steps to Follow

1. Cut out the bear writing form. Mount the finished stories on brown construction paper. Trim, leaving a 1" (2.5 cm) border of brown.

2. Make the bear claws.
   - Students cut claws from the meat tray. Have some examples cut to show possible shapes before students begin cutting.
   - Punch a hole in the top of each claw.

3. Make fur beads.
   - Put a line of glue along the smooth side of a fur rectangle.
   - Roll the other side to the glue to form a tube or bead.
   - Hold the tube gently until the glue sets.

4. String the claw between two of the fur beads.
   - Put a fur bead on the string.
   - Add a claw.
   - Finish with a second fur bead.

5. Punch a hole in the writing form and attach the bear claw decoration as shown.

Bear Writing Form

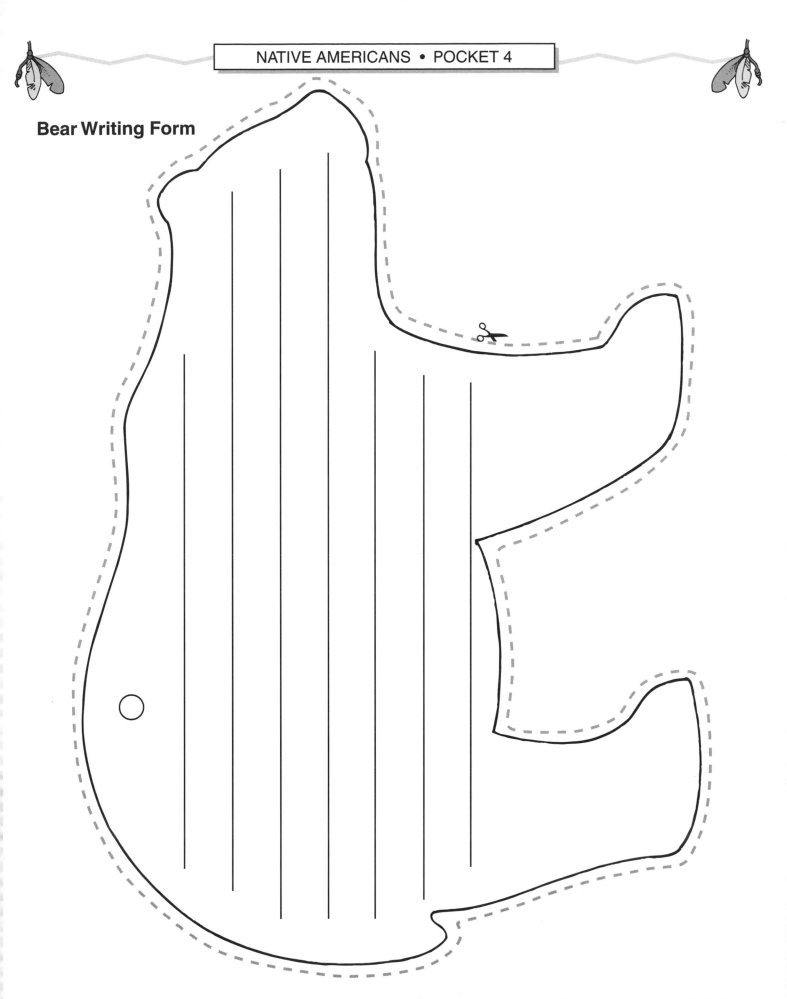

Note: Reproduce this page and page 61 to label each of the four pockets of the Native Americans book.

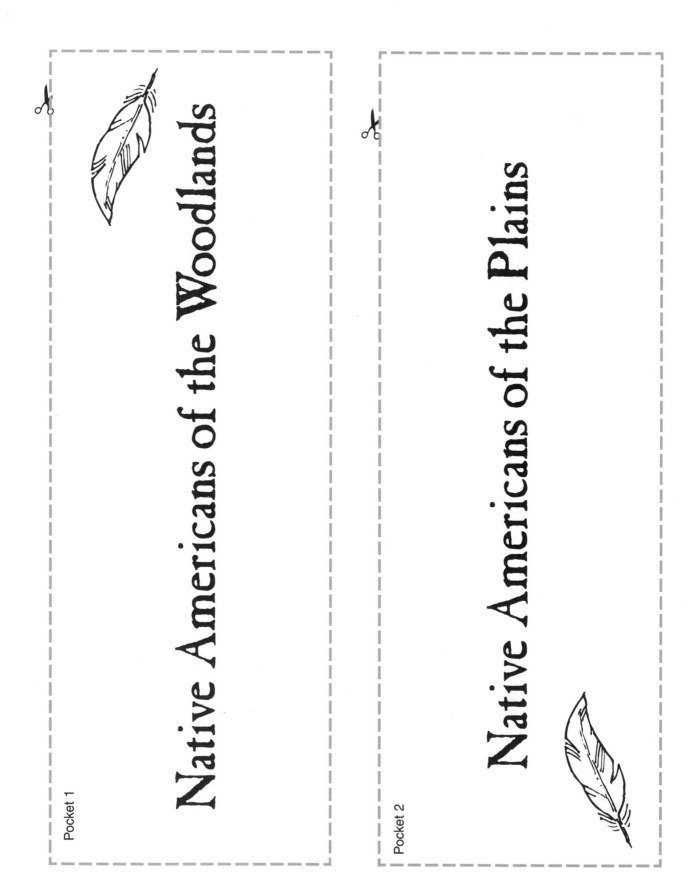

Pocket 1

Native Americans of the Woodlands

Pocket 2

Native Americans of the Plains

Pocket 3

Native Americans of the Southwest

Pocket 4

Native Americans of the Northwest Coast and the Far North

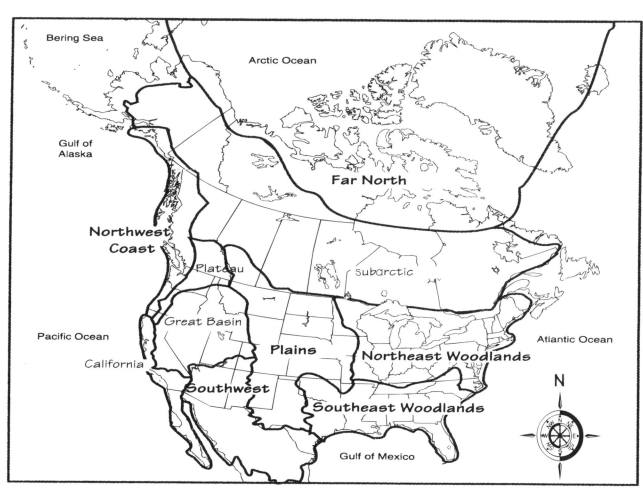

Northwest & Far North

cedar
totem poles
salmon
whales
potlatch
caribou
polar bear
dogsled
kayaks
igloos
Inuit

Plains

buffalo
tipi
travois
moccasins
shields
bow
arrows
parfleche

Southwest

sheep
hogans
weavers
Hopi
Navajo
Pueblo
mesas

Northeast & Southeast

maize
swamps
squash
pumpkins
straw
longhouse
wigwam
canoe
deerskin
birch bark

Name: _____

The Food Pyramid

The United States Department of Agriculture (USDA) introduced the Food Pyramid to help people choose foods for a healthy diet. It is really a graph designed to show the importance of variety, proportion, and moderation. Teach your students about the food pyramid with the activities in this pocket book.

The Food Pyramid

BIBLIOGRAPHY

ABC Yummy by Lisa Jahn-Clough; Houghton Mifflin, 1997.

Bread, Bread, Bread by Ann Morris; Mulberry Books, 1993.

Five Kids and a Monkey Solve the Great Cupcake Caper: A Learning Adventure About Nutrition and Exercise by Nina Riccio; Creative Attic, 1997.

Gregory, the Terrible Eater by Mitchell Sharmat; Simon & Schuster, 1980.

Growing Vegetable Soup by Lois Ehlert; Harcourt Brace, 1987.

Healthy Snacks for Kids by Penny Warner; Bristol Pub Enterprises, 1996.

Nutrition: What's in the Food We Eat by Dorothy Hinshaw Patent; Holiday House, 1992.

The Race Against Junk Food by Brian Silberman et al. (editors); Hcom Inc, 1997.

POCKET 1

The Food Pyramid
Grains   **page 69**
After learning about the foods in this group,
students write or draw to show their favorites.

Slice It Right!   **pages 70–72**
Add your own recipes to this little shape
book.

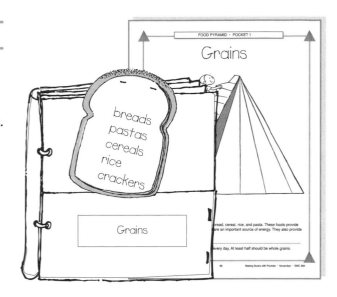

POCKET 2

The Food Pyramid
Vegetables   **page 73**
After learning about the foods in this group,
students write or draw to show their favorites.

Vegetable Fun   **page 74**
Pick vegetable names from a list and write
about your favorite.

POCKET 3

The Food Pyramid
Fruits   **page 75**
After learning about the foods in this group,
students write or draw to show their
favorites.

Fruit Collage   **pages 76–79**
This colorful collage is also a word bank
and a recipe poster.

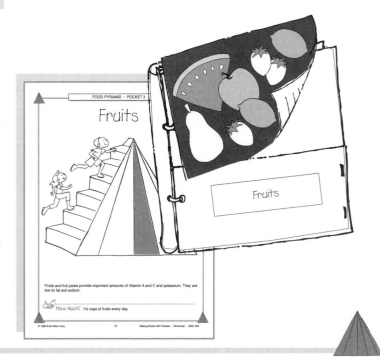

POCKET 4

The Food Pyramid
Milk   page 80
After learning about the foods in this group, students write or draw to show their favorites.

The Big Cheese   pages 81 and 82
Inside its holes, this hunk of cheese is full of ideas.

Reading Labels   pages 83 and 84
Learn to read the nutrition facts on food labels.

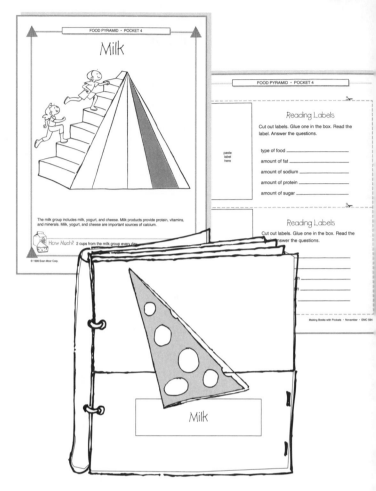

POCKET 5

The Food Pyramid
Meat and Beans   page 85
After learning about the foods in this group, students write or draw to show their favorites.

Basic Barbeque   pages 86 and 87
Make this model of a barbeque to hold your meat and beans group lists and recipes.

Building a Healthy Meal pages 88 and 89
Students plan and show a balanced meal.

Make the cover for this pocket book after you have studied each of the food groups in the food pyramid. The cover will then serve as an assessment tool to see if students can identify and correctly group different foods.

Materials

- construction paper
  background—orange, 12" (30.5 cm) square
- pyramid and label patterns on page 68, reproduced for each student
- crayons
- scissors
- glue
- strips of yarn
- hole punch

Steps to Follow

1. Cut out and glue the pyramid to the construction paper square. Color the letters, using a variety of colors.

2. Cut out and glue the labels below the correct sections.

3. Punch holes and bind the pockets together with strips of yarn.

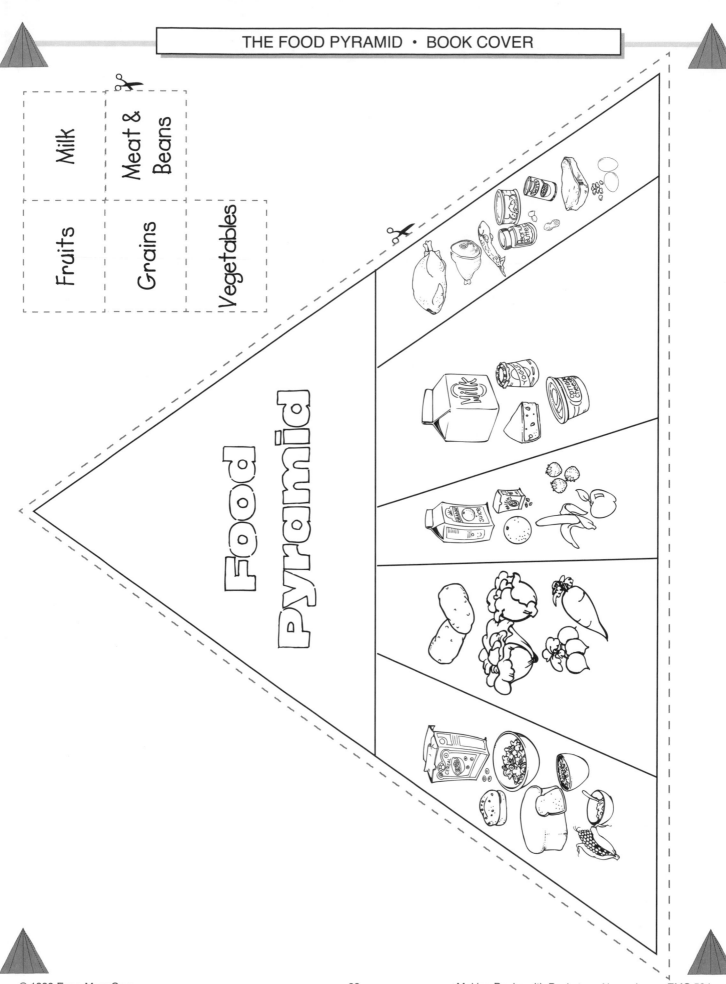

Milk

Meat & Beans

Fruits

Grains

Vegetables

Food Pyramid

Grains

The grains group includes whole-grain bread, cereal, rice, and pasta. These foods provide complex carbohydrates (starches), which are an important source of energy. They also provide vitamins, minerals, and fiber.

 How Much? 6 oz. of grains every day (at least half should be whole grains).

Slice It Right!

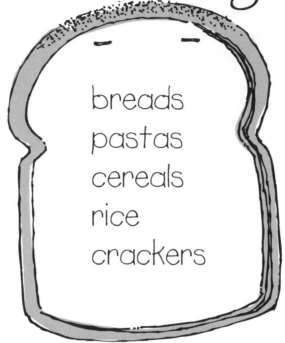

breads
pastas
cereals
rice
crackers

Use this slice of bread to list all of the members of the grains food group.

Materials

- crust—brown, 9" x 12" (23 x 30.5 cm) construction paper
- bread slice writing form on page 71 and recipe on page 72, reproduced for each student
- scissors
- cornmeal
- glue

Steps to Follow

1. Cut out the writing form and the recipe.

2. Lay the writing form on the brown "crust" and trace around it. Cut the brown paper ½" (1.25 cm) larger than the line drawn.

3. Spread glue along the top edge of the crust. Sprinkle cornmeal on the glue. Shake off the excess. Let the crust dry.

4. List foods that are part of the grains food group on the writing form. Add more pages as needed.

5. Staple the form and the recipe to the crust.

Bread Slice Writing Form

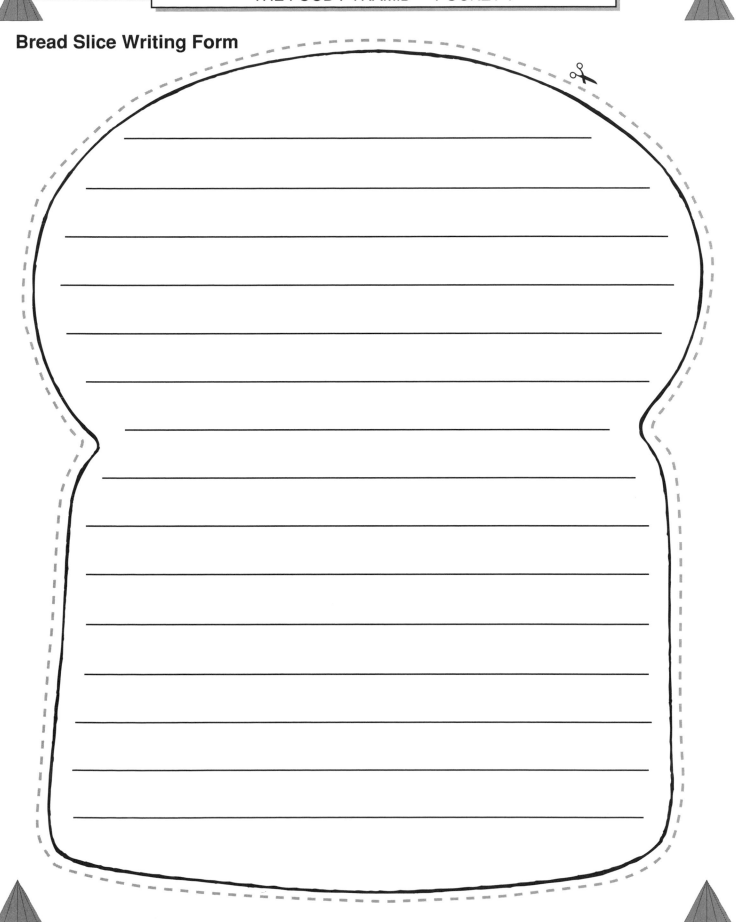

Bread Slice Recipe

My Favorite Sandwich

Tell how to make your favorite sandwich.
Be sure to use whole wheat bread.

_____

_____

_____

_____

_____

_____

_____

_____

_____

_____

Vegetables

Vegetables provide vitamins and minerals such as iron and magnesium. They are naturally low in fat and also provide fiber.

How Much? 2 ½ cups of vegetables every day.

Name: _____

Circle all the vegetables you can find in this list.

Vegetable Fun

celery	chocolate	asparagus
sweet potatoes	french fries	cabbage
apples	hamburger	oranges
broccoli	carrots	green beans

Write about your favorite vegetable. How do you like to eat it?

_____

_____

_____

_____

_____

_____

_____

         Making Books with Pockets • November • EMC 594

Fruits

Fruits and fruit juices provide important amounts of vitamins A and C and potassium. They are low in fat and sodium.

 How Much? 1½ cups of fruits every day.

Fruit Collage

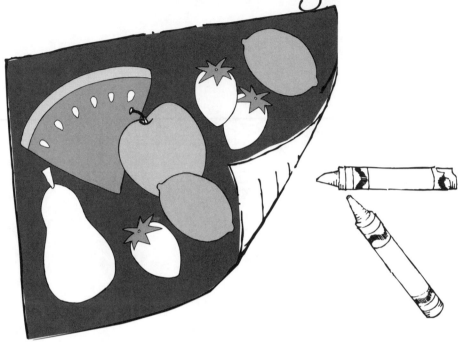

A bright, colorful collage of fruit with a recipe is a great way to remember to include at least five servings a day.

Materials

- fruit patterns on pages 77 and 78, reproduced on white construction paper for each student
- forms on page 79, reproduced for each student
- 9" x 12" (23 x 30.5 cm) black construction paper
- glue
- scissors
- crayons

Steps to Follow

1. Color the fruit patterns. Encourage students to make the colors dark and vibrant. Try putting folded newspaper under the paper when you color.

2. Cut out the fruits. Glue them to the construction paper.

3. Cut out the list form and the recipe on page 79. Fill in the list. Glue the list and the recipe to the back of the collage.

Fruit Patterns

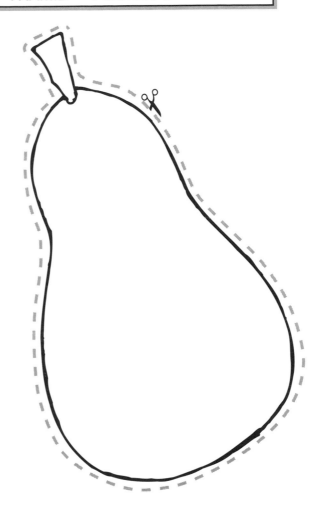

Making Books with Pockets • November • EMC 594

Glue to the back of the fruit collage.

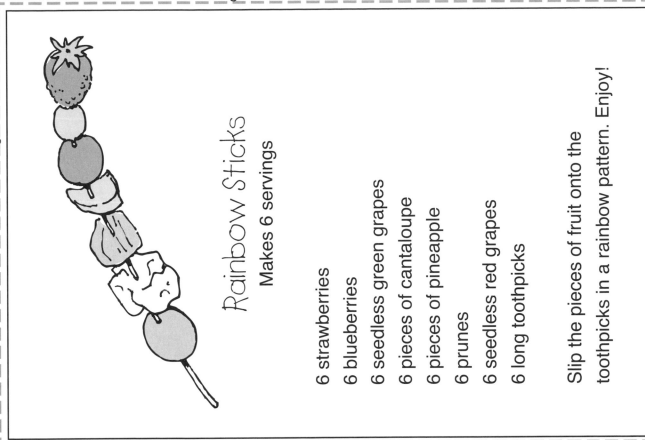

Rainbow Sticks

Makes 6 servings

6 strawberries

6 blueberries

6 seedless green grapes

6 pieces of cantaloupe

6 pieces of pineapple

6 prunes

6 seedless red grapes

6 long toothpicks

Slip the pieces of fruit onto the toothpicks in a rainbow pattern. Enjoy!

My List of Fruits

Milk

The milk group includes milk, yogurt, and cheese. Milk products provide protein, vitamins, and minerals. Milk, yogurt, and cheese are important sources of calcium.

 How Much? 3 cups from the milk group every day.

The Big Cheese

This hunk of cheese is full of ideas inside its holes.

Materials

- orange or yellow, 9" x 12" (23 x 30.5 cm) construction paper
- list form on page 82, reproduced for each student
- scissors
- stapler

Steps to Follow

1. Fold the construction paper in half crosswise.

2. Show students how to gently fold the paper in several places and cut circles from the wedge. Then have students cut holes in their cheese wedge folder.

3. Have students cut out and complete the My Favorites writing forms.

4. Brainstorm and list foods in the milk group. Students copy the list onto their forms.

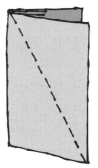

Cut on the diagonal as shown to make the cheese wedge.

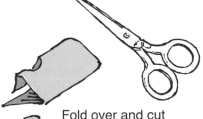

Fold over and cut out several circles.

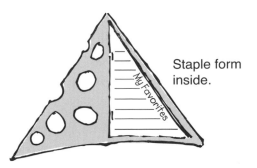

Staple form inside.

List Form

Use these forms for students to list and write about their favorite kinds of milk products.

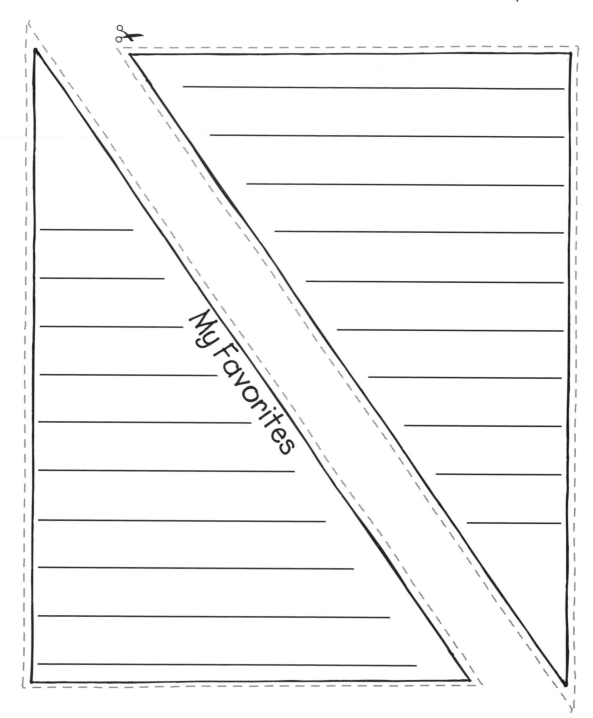

My Favorites

Reading Labels

Help your students develop an awareness of the information included on food labels. Do this activity as a whole class, assign it as an at-home family project, or have individual students analyze food products.

Materials

- recording form on page 84, reproduced for each student and made into a transparency for demonstration
- transparency of a nutrition fact label from a common food such as cereal
- food containers

Steps to Follow

1. Using a sample food container with a nutrition fact label, demonstrate how to find the information that is called for on the recording form. Fill in the transparency with information from your sample.

2. Have students complete a form after reading the nutrition facts on another food container.

Reading Labels

Cut out labels. Glue one in the box. Read the label. Answer the questions.

paste
label
here

type of food _____

amount of fat _____

amount of sodium _____

amount of protein _____

amount of sugar _____

Reading Labels

Cut out labels. Glue one in the box. Read the label. Answer the questions.

paste
label
here

type of food _____

amount of fat _____

amount of sodium _____

amount of protein _____

amount of sugar _____

Meat and Beans

The meat and beans group includes meat, poultry, fish, eggs, nuts, seeds, peas, and beans. These foods supply protein, vitamins, and minerals.

 How Much? 5 oz. from the meat and beans group every day.

Basic Barbeque

Lift the lid on the BBQ to find a recipe and a list of foods that are part of the meat and beans group.

Materials

- construction paper
  BBQ—light gray, 12" x 18" (30.5 x 45.5 cm)
  rack—dark gray, 8" x 8½" (20 x 21.5 cm)
  charcoal—24 black, 2" (5 cm) squares
  handle—black, 4" x 2" (10 x 5 cm)
  meats—multicolored scraps

- scissors
- glue
- red or orange crayon
- recipe and list form on page 87, reproduced for each student

Steps to Follow

1. Fold the light gray paper in half to make a folder.

2. Round the edges as shown.

3. Round the top edges of the black rectangle. Cut out the middle as shown to make a handle. Glue the handle to the BBQ.

folder *handle*

4. Round the corners of the black squares. Add a crayon scribble of red or orange to the top of each square. Place the charcoal inside the folder and glue in place.

5. Fold the dark gray paper in half. Cut slits from the folded edge to about 1" (2.5 cm) from the open edges. Unfold the paper. Cut out every other strip to make the BBQ grill. Glue the grill over the charcoal.

6. Cut the construction paper scraps into meat shapes such as hamburgers, hot dogs, pork chops, and drumsticks. Glue the meats to the grill.

7. Brainstorm and list items in the meat and beans group. Have students copy the list onto their forms.

8. Glue the recipe and the form to the inside top of the BBQ.

Busy-Day Burritos

Makes 4 servings

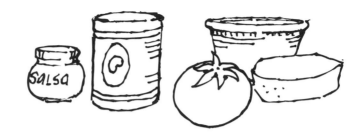

4 flour tortillas
1 can of vegetarian refried beans
4–6 cooked chicken strips
1 tomato, chopped
2 oz (57 g) of cheddar cheese, shredded
salsa and sour cream, to taste

Lay tortillas on a flat surface.
Spread refried beans on top.
Place chicken strips on top of the beans.
Sprinkle with chopped tomato and cheese.
Roll the tortillas.

Microwave about 40 seconds or until the beans are hot and the cheese
is melted.

Building a Healthy Meal

Here's a chance to put together all you've learned to plan a healthy meal.

Materials

- 12" x 9" (30.5 x 23 cm) construction paper
- planning form on page 89, reproduced for each student
- drawing paper
- paper napkin
- plastic fork, knife, and spoon
- paper plate
- crayons or marking pens
- scissors
- glue

Steps to Follow

1. Plan a balanced, healthy meal. Record the menu on the planning form.

2. Draw and cut out foods included in the meal. Glue the food cutouts to the plate.

3. Using the paper as a placemat, create a place setting. Glue the plate, utensils, and napkin in place.

4. Glue the planning form on the back of the placemat.

Name: _____

Building a Meal with a Healthy Variety of Foods

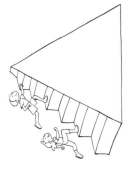

The Menu for My Meal

Planning Form

Plan your meal. Write down each thing you will eat. Check to see that you have some foods from each part of the pyramid. Add foods so that your meal is balanced.

1. Grains
2. Vegetables
3. Fruits
4. Milk
5. Meat and Beans

Note: Reproduce this page and page 91 to label each of the five pockets in the Food Pyramid book.

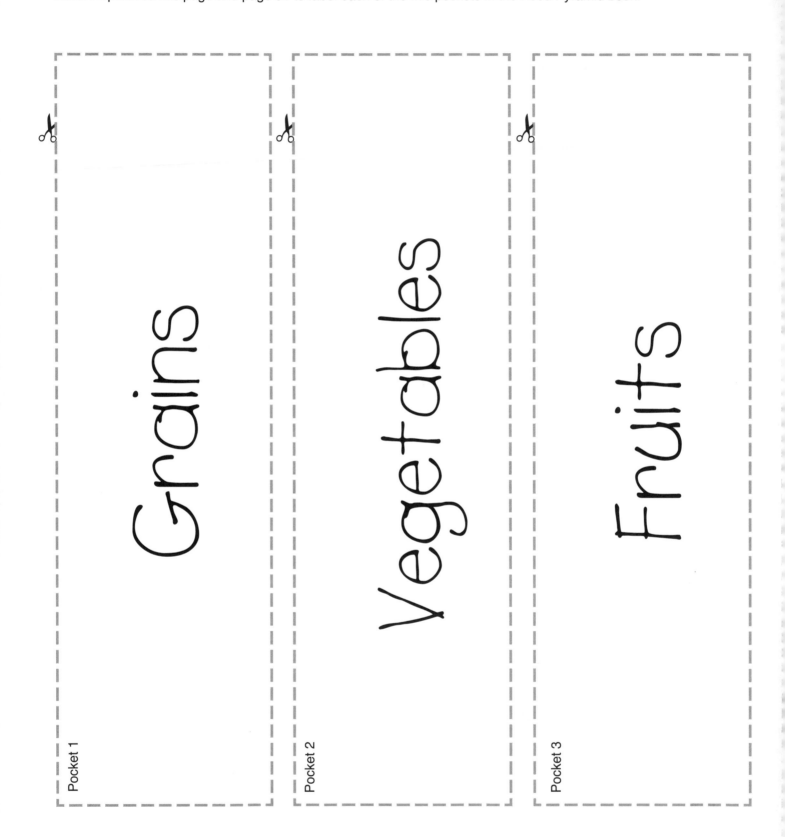

Grains

Pocket 1

Vegetables

Pocket 2

Fruits

Pocket 3

Pocket 4

Milk

Pocket 5

Meat and Beans

Grains	Vegetables	Fruit	Milk	Meat and Beans

breads	lettuce	bananas	milk	beef
cereals	broccoli	oranges	yogurt	pork
rice	cucumbers	apples	ice cream	fish
tortillas	green beans	grapes	cheese	lamb
crackers	carrots	kiwis		nuts
wheat	potatoes	pears		beans
pasta	spinach	strawberries		steak
	corn	plums		hamburger
		watermelon		chicken
		grapefruit		eggs

Making Books with Pockets • November • EMC 594

Name: _____

Bulletin Board Bonanza

Mr. Turkey—page 95

This perky turkey is a wonderful community classroom project. It may be such a hit that your students will want to keep it up when November is over. You can always add a stocking hat and a red nose!

> Write things that you are thankful for on the index cards, punch holes in the cards, and display them on the board. Here are several suggestions for how to do this:
>
> - Ask all students to write at the same time and then fill the board with thankful ideas.
>
> - Choose one student each day to tell what he or she is thankful for. You write the student's thoughts, and post the card.
>
> - Have students ask school personnel what they are thankful for and then record the ideas on the cards to post.

A Fabulous Food Pyramid—page 96

Using real food containers to create a three-dimensional food pyramid will not only help students categorize foods but will also encourage reading environmental print. This bulletin board represents an important connection between what students learn in school and their everyday lives at home.

Use this bulletin board as a catalyst for discussions.

Which food group contains the foods you like most?
Let's see what food groups were represented by today's lunch.

Mr. Turkey

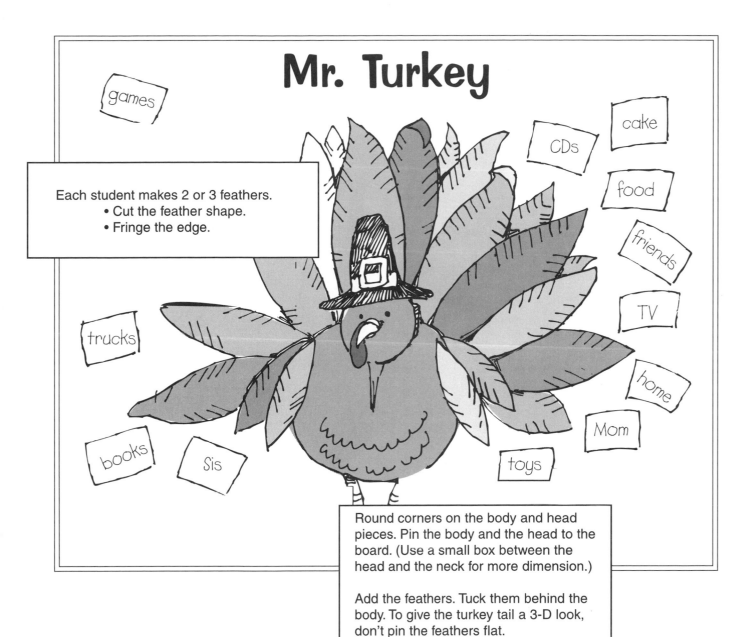

Each student makes 2 or 3 feathers.
- Cut the feather shape.
- Fringe the edge.

Round corners on the body and head pieces. Pin the body and the head to the board. (Use a small box between the head and the neck for more dimension.)

Add the feathers. Tuck them behind the body. To give the turkey tail a 3-D look, don't pin the feathers flat.

Add details—beak, wattle, eyes, feet, a Pilgrim's hat.

Materials

- construction paper
  feathers—assorted colors, 4" x 18" (10 x 45.5 cm)
  body—brown, 12" (30.5 cm) square
  head—brown, 5" (13 cm) square
  beak—yellow or orange, 10" x 4" (25.5 x 10 cm)
  wattle—red, 6" x 3" (15 x 7.5 cm)
  feet—black, 9" x 12" (23 x 30.5 cm)
  eyes—scraps of white and black
  hat—black, 4" x 3" (10 x 7.5 cm)

- scissors
- paste
- pins
- 3" x 5" (7.5 x 13 cm) index cards
- hole punch

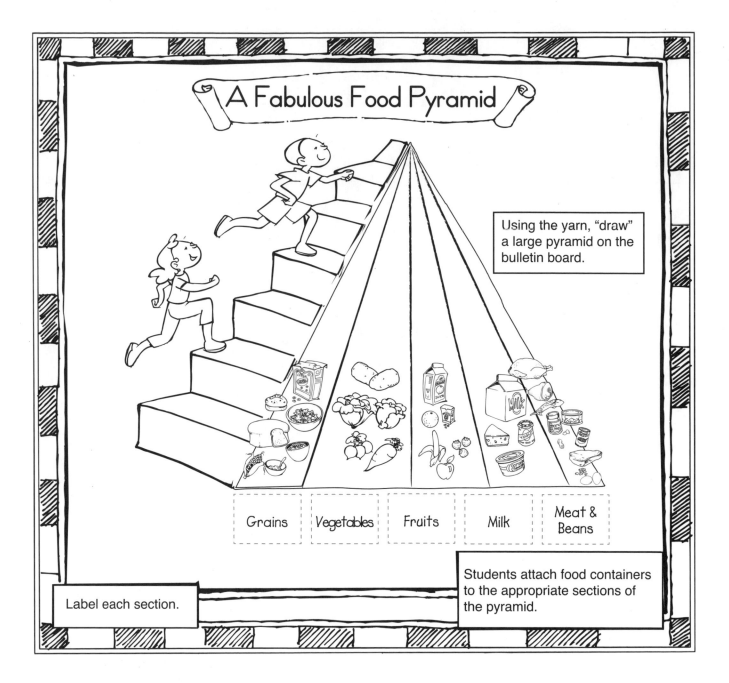

A Fabulous Food Pyramid

Using the yarn, "draw" a large pyramid on the bulletin board.

Grains | Vegetables | Fruits | Milk | Meat & Beans

Label each section.

Students attach food containers to the appropriate sections of the pyramid.

Materials

- heavy yarn
- food group labels (You could use the pocket labels on pages 90 and 91.)
- clean, empty food containers
- pins and tape